HOW NOT TO BE A CEO

S J DEL MONTE

S J DEL MONTE

Copyright © 2024 S J Del Monte

All rights reserved

The characters and events portrayed in this book are fictitious. Any similarity to real persons, living or dead, is coincidental and not intended by the author.

No part of this book may be reproduced, or stored in a retrieval system, or transmitted in any form or by any means, electronic, mechanical, photocopying, recording, or otherwise, without express written permission of the publisher.

ISBN: 9798329536140
Imprint: Independently published

Cover design by: Art Painter
Library of Congress Control Number: 2018675309
Printed in the United States of America

ISBN: 9798329536140
Imprint: Independently published

SEBASTIAN JDEL MONTE

HOW NOT TO:
BE A CEO

BY S J DEL MONTE

© S J Del Monte

Dedicated to anyone who had to suffer the pain of having a terrible boss...

PROLOGUE

This book emerged from years of frustration working across various sectors—from big corporations to small businesses, start-ups, and scale-ups. What tied many of them together were managers who treated these companies as their personal playgrounds.

Like many aspiring graduates, I began my career at the bottom of the ladder. Months of applying for countless entry-level positions, which demanded only a degree but rejected me due to lack of experience, planted seeds of frustration early on. From these experiences, I learned the importance of honest communication, realistic goal-setting, and the value of a supportive team.

Decades and numerous job changes later, as I moved into managerial roles reporting directly to CEOs, those seeds grew into a dense forest of dissatisfaction. I observed firsthand the common mistakes that many leaders make, often driven by ego or a desire to impress. If this scenario sounds all too familiar, keep reading…

1.
TIME IS MONEY: WHY WASTE IT ON MISTAKES WHILE YOU CAN LEARN FROM OTHERS?

Whether you took a leap of faith from your 9 to 5 or grew up believing you were destined to be a great leader, starting or growing a company can be daunting. There are many resources available to help, but they often miss the pitfalls that aspiring CEOs might encounter. You can learn about tested methods for a successful product launch, efficient time management with Gantt charts, and data analysis to attract investors or customers. However, what about the often-overlooked soft skills needed to build and maintain a dedicated team willing to join you on this journey?

I will highlight where many CEOs I have met went wrong in their management styles, leading to their or their company's downfall. Use this book as a guide to navigate the landscape and avoid costly mistakes that could have serious consequences.

Through years of working alongside CEOs across various sectors and company sizes, I have identified common mistakes that many leaders make. Instead of recounting glorious success stories (there are plenty of biographies for that), I have decided to create a guide that maps out the pitfalls, cliff edges, and landmines for new and existing CEOs. This guide is designed for those who are just starting their journey or looking to elevate their leadership to the next level, helping them avoid costly mistakes and navigate the challenges ahead.

Everyone has a unique way of working depending on factors such as their character, appetite for risk, and motivations. In today's rapidly changing corporate landscape, what works for one person does not always work for another. It is important to focus on your strengths when planning your journey. Taking a pioneering approach and figuring out your own path might sound riskier than following a pre-approved strategy; however, it could provide an edge that makes you stand out in the overcrowded commercial world. Instead of following in the footsteps of someone who made it to the top, who almost certainly made and learned from their own mistakes, you could learn the same lessons without repeating them. Success stories usually omit these valuable lessons behind achievements, as they are not as attractive as a simplified success narrative. Rather than romanticising the struggles and casting them as a heroic journey, use these insights as road signs to warn you about sharp bends and hidden dips, leaving your mind free to focus on what truly matters—your journey.

2.
THE HOLLOW TITLE

In the wild world of startups and small businesses, titles often denote influence and authority. Among these, none commands as much respect as that of CEO. This designation symbolises power, achievement, and the fact that you probably have a really nice business card. But does the reality match the perception?

For many aspiring entrepreneurs, the allure of the CEO title is irresistible. It represents the pinnacle of success, the culmination of years of hard work, and perhaps the promise of a corner office. Yet, behind the title lies a critical truth: true leadership is not granted by a title; it is earned through actions, integrity, and a commitment to excellence (and maybe a few all-nighters).

THE ILLUSION OF POWER

Sure, the title of CEO can open doors and command initial respect, but it also sets high expectations. Team members may initially defer to the authority of a new CEO, but without demonstrated capability and a track record of sound decisions, this deference quickly turns into doubt and criticism. It's like being the captain of a ship with no map or compass—people are bound to jump overboard eventually.

Case Study: The Cost of Overconfidence

Consider the story of a new CEO at a promising tech startup. Enthusiastic and confident, they assumed their title would naturally lead to respect and compliance. However, their tendency to micromanage and lack of transparent communication led to frustration among team members. Innovation stalled, and key talent left for competitors who offered a more empowering work environment. This example underscores that true influence comes from merit and genuine leadership, not just a title (and certainly not just a fancy office).

THE RESPONSIBILITY GAP

Adopting the CEO title without the necessary skills and mindset can lead to chaos and mismanagement. Critical decisions might be delayed or made impulsively, causing inefficiencies, missed opportunities, and financial losses. Effective CEOs must balance strategic oversight and operational management. Without a well-defined strategic vision, the company may lack direction, leading to confusion and misaligned efforts among team members.

Example: The Retail Startup

Take, for example, a retail startup that rapidly expanded without a clear strategic plan. The CEO's impulsive decision-making and lack of resource management led to overextended finances and uncoordinated efforts across departments. Eventually, the company faced severe financial strain, highlighting the importance of strategic foresight and careful planning in leadership. Who knew running a company wasn't just about giving inspiring speeches?

MISALIGNMENT OF EXPECTATIONS

Mismanaging expectations can harm relationships with investors, customers, and employees. Investors may become disillusioned if promised growth and profitability do not materialise, leading to a loss of support. Customers may lose confidence if products or services do not meet their expectations, affecting sales and reputation. Similarly, employees may become disengaged if promised opportunities for growth are unfulfilled, leading to high turnover and a loss of talent.

Example: The Software Company

A well-known example involves a software company that overpromised features in its upcoming release. When the product fell short, customer dissatisfaction led to a surge in negative reviews and a decline in sales. Meanwhile, employees felt misled about their roles in the product development process, resulting in decreased morale and increased turnover. This scenario illustrates how aligning expectations with achievable outcomes is critical for maintaining trust and loyalty (and avoiding angry mobs with pitchforks).

LACK OF DIRECTION

Without a clear vision and strategic direction, a company may struggle to adapt to changing market conditions and capitalise on emerging opportunities. A clear vision serves as the company's North Star, guiding every decision and action. When this vision is absent or poorly communicated, the entire organisation can suffer from a sense of aimlessness. Employees may be uncertain about the company's goals, leading to fragmented efforts and a lack of cohesion in achieving objectives.

Example: The Healthcare Startup

For instance, a healthcare startup failed to articulate its vision and strategic goals, resulting in disparate projects that didn't align with a cohesive strategy. This lack of direction caused confusion among employees and diluted the company's market impact. Eventually, competitors with clearer strategies overtook them, demonstrating the vital role of a well-communicated vision in driving company success. It's like trying to win a game of charades with a mime—good luck with that.

NO ONE IS A ONE-MAN CANOE

Even the mightiest CEOs aren't lone rangers. They're more like captains of a pirate ship—without a loyal crew, they're just shouting orders at seagulls. CEOs should choose their team wisely, look after their team, and empower them. A well-chosen team can make or break a company. Remember, you're only as good as the people around you. Treat your team well, and they'll sail with you through stormy seas.

Example: The Captain and Crew

A startup CEO once believed they could handle everything solo—strategy, operations, even brewing the office coffee. Predictably, things went south faster than a snowbird in January. Only after assembling a competent and motivated team did the ship start to right itself. The moral of the story? No one sails alone. Even pirates have first mates.

Illustration: The Canoe and the Crew

To illustrate, consider the story of a CEO of a budding e-commerce platform. This CEO initially believed they had to oversee every single aspect of the company to ensure success. Their days were filled with meetings, product reviews, customer service calls, and even handling social media. The CEO was spread so thin that their effectiveness waned. It wasn't until they hired and trusted a team of experts—each excelling in their respective fields—that the company began to thrive. The team, feeling empowered and trusted, brought innovative solutions and efficiencies the CEO had never considered. The lesson? Even the best ships need a crew to sail smoothly.

FORMED, NOT JUST MADE DECISIONS

Decisions should be formed, not just made. Like a fine wine, they need time, proper information, and a bit of finesse. Basing decisions on sound understanding rather than gut feelings or luck ensures they're more likely to succeed. Nothing annoys your learned staff more than a CEO who ignores professional advice just to please their own ego. It's like telling your GPS you know a better route during rush hour—it never ends well.

Case in Point: The Overconfident Navigator

Imagine a CEO who constantly disregards the advice of their seasoned marketing team, choosing instead to follow their "gut feeling." Unsurprisingly, the company's campaigns flop, budgets overrun, and the team's morale hits rock bottom. The lesson? Trust your experts—they've got more than just intuition; they've got knowledge and experience.

Example: The Intuitive CEO

Consider the example of a CEO of a tech startup. This CEO thought they knew better than their experienced engineering team and decided to launch a product update based on their "gut feeling." Despite their team's data showing potential issues, the CEO pushed forward. The update was a disaster, causing system crashes and customer backlash. Had the CEO listened to their team and formed their decision based on their input, the fiasco could have been avoided. The moral? Data and expertise trump gut feelings, every time.

PERSUASION OVER RANK-PULLING

If a CEO cannot persuade others with a reasoned argument and has to pull rank, they should question their decisions. Resorting to authority instead of logic is a sign that something might be amiss. If your idea can't stand on its own merit, perhaps it needs a bit more thought—or maybe it's just a terrible idea. Persuasion is the true mark of a leader; rank-pulling is the mark of a tyrant (and nobody likes a tyrant).

Scenario: The Rank-Pulling Fiasco

Consider a CEO who regularly silences dissent by pulling rank, insisting their way is the only way. This might work in the short term, but eventually, the best and brightest will flee, leaving behind yes-men and a company on the brink of collapse. If you need to rely on your title to get things done, it's time to rethink your approach.

Example: The Persuasive Leader

Take, for example, the CEO of a growing fashion brand. This CEO often dismissed their team's innovative ideas, resorting to "because I said so" tactics. This approach stifled creativity and drove away the most talented designers who felt undervalued. In contrast, when they began encouraging open discussions and rational debates, the team felt empowered, and the company flourished with fresh, market-leading designs. Lesson learned: Lead with logic, not titles.

RISK OF FAILURE

Ultimately, businesses led by CEOs who lack the necessary skills and mindset are at a higher risk of failure. Poor decision-making, ineffective communication, and a lack of strategic planning can result in losses, dwindling market share, and damage to the company's reputation. Investors may withdraw support, creditors may call in debts, and employees may seek opportunities elsewhere, hastening the company's decline.

Reflection: Learning from Pitfalls

Reflecting on these potential pitfalls is essential. For example, a financial services firm under inexperienced leadership saw rapid decline due to mismanaged resources and strategic missteps. Investors pulled out, and top talent left for more stable opportunities. This cautionary tale highlights the importance of continuous self-improvement, seeking mentorship, and remaining adaptable to the evolving business environment.

CONCLUSION

In essence, the CEO title is not just a symbol of power; it carries significant responsibilities that must be met with competence and integrity. Sustainable success in the CEO role is built on a blend of respect, trust, and genuine leadership qualities. By embracing continuous self-improvement, fostering open communication, and developing robust strategic plans, aspiring entrepreneurs can avoid the traps of hollow titles and build a foundation for lasting success in the challenging world of startups and small businesses. Because at the end of the day, it's not just about having the title; it's about earning it every single day (and maybe surviving a few office pranks along the way).

Additional Reflections

Remember, the role of a CEO is not just to lead, but to inspire and empower those around them. A great CEO understands the value of their team, makes informed decisions, and persuades through reason. By embracing humility, fostering collaboration, and prioritising transparency, you can build a stronger, more resilient organisation capable of achieving sustainable success.

3.
THE PITFALLS OF EGO-DRIVEN LEADERSHIP

A common mistake among new CEOs is the belief that their desire to succeed is stronger than that of their staff. This mindset can lead to a series of detrimental behaviours: pulling rank unnecessarily, insisting on always being right, and dismissing the contributions of others. These actions can alienate employees, foster an environment of silos, and breed dishonesty within the organisation.

ALIENATING STAFF

When a CEO continually asserts their authority, it sends a clear message to the team: "Your opinions and efforts are secondary to mine." This approach demoralises employees, leading to decreased engagement and productivity. Staff members may feel undervalued and disrespected, causing a loss of motivation and a decrease in job satisfaction. Over time, this can result in high turnover rates as talented individuals seek workplaces where their contributions are recognised and appreciated.

Case Study: The Cost of Overconfidence

Consider the case of a CEO who took pride in making unilateral decisions, believing their strategic vision was superior. This CEO often dismissed team suggestions, leading to a significant disconnect between leadership and staff. The result? Critical information was withheld, projects were delayed, and ultimately, the company suffered financially as key employees left for competitors.

Humour Insert: Let's be honest, thinking you're the smartest person in the room is a surefire way to end up talking to an empty room.

ENCOURAGING SILOS

An ego-driven leadership style often creates silos within the organisation. When a CEO believes they are the only one with the right answers, departments begin to work in isolation. This lack of collaboration can cripple a company's ability to innovate and adapt. Silos prevent the free flow of information and ideas, leading to inefficiencies and missed opportunities.

Example: The Dangers of Isolation

In one technology firm, the CEO's insistence on making all major decisions without consulting other departments led to a lack of coordination between teams. Marketing campaigns were launched without input from the product development team, resulting in misaligned messaging and lost sales. The company's growth stagnated as internal divisions deepened, making it difficult to respond to market changes effectively.

Humour Insert: Imagine trying to play a team sport where everyone has their own ball and no one passes. Welcome to the world of silos.

BREEDING DISHONESTY

A CEO who is always right and dismisses dissenting views can inadvertently encourage dishonesty. Employees, fearing retribution or dismissal of their ideas, may choose to withhold information or provide false feedback. This lack of transparency can have serious consequences, as leadership is left making decisions based on incomplete or inaccurate data.

Scenario: The High Cost of False Feedback

Imagine a scenario where a CEO's aggressive stance discourages honest communication. In a manufacturing company, workers noticed flaws in the production process but feared raising the issue due to the CEO's dismissive attitude. The result was a series of defective products reaching the market, leading to recalls, financial losses, and damage to the company's reputation.

Humour Insert: If you're creating an environment where people are afraid to speak the truth, you're essentially driving your company with a blindfold on.

BUILDING A COLLABORATIVE CULTURE

To avoid these pitfalls, CEOs must adopt a more inclusive and collaborative leadership style. Here are key strategies to consider:

1. Empower Your Team: Trust in the capabilities of your staff and encourage their input. Create an environment where employees feel valued and heard.

2. Foster Collaboration: Break down silos by promoting cross-functional teams and open communication channels. Ensure all departments are aligned and working towards common goals.

3. Encourage Honesty: Build a culture of transparency where employees can share their insights and concerns without fear. Recognise and reward honesty and integrity.

4.Practice Humility: Acknowledge that you do not have all the answers. Be open to learning from your team and admit when you are wrong.

Illustration: The Canoe and the Crew

Think of your company as a canoe. If only one person is paddling, you'll go in circles. But with a team, you can navigate through rapids and reach your destination faster and more efficiently. A CEO who understands this will foster a collaborative environment where every paddle stroke counts.

Example: The Empowered Team

Consider the story of a CEO of a budding e-commerce platform. Initially, this CEO believed they had to oversee every single aspect of the company to ensure success. Their days were filled with meetings, product reviews, customer service calls, and even handling social media. The CEO was spread so thin that their effectiveness waned. It wasn't until they hired and trusted a team of experts—each excelling in their respective fields—that the company began to thrive. The team, feeling empowered and trusted, brought innovative solutions and efficiencies the CEO had never considered. The lesson? Even the best ships need a crew to sail smoothly.

FORMED, NOT JUST MADE DECISIONS

Decisions should be formed, not just made. Like a fine wine, they need time, proper information, and a bit of finesse. Basing decisions on sound understanding rather than gut feelings or luck ensures they're more likely to succeed. Nothing annoys your learned staff more than a CEO who ignores professional advice just to please their own ego. It's like telling your GPS you know a better route during rush hour—it never ends well.

Case in Point: The Overconfident Navigator

Imagine being a CEO who constantly disregards the advice of your seasoned marketing team, choosing instead to follow your "gut feeling." Unsurprisingly, the company's campaigns flop, budgets overrun, and the team's morale hits rock bottom. The lesson? Trust your experts—they've got more than just intuition; they've got knowledge and experience.

Example: The Gut-Driven Decision

Consider the scenario of a CEO overseeing a tech startup's major product launch. Ignoring the advice and data provided by the experienced marketing team, the CEO insisted on a bold, gut-driven advertising strategy. Despite warnings of potential mismatches with the target audience, the CEO pushed forward. The campaign flopped, failing to attract the expected interest and resulting in significant financial losses. If the CEO had considered the team's insights and data, the company could have launched a more effective and resonant campaign. The lesson? Trusting data and expertise leads to better outcomes than relying solely on intuition.

PERSUASION OVER RANK-PULLING

If a CEO cannot persuade others with a reasoned argument and has to pull rank, they should question their decisions. Resorting to authority instead of logic is a sign that something might be amiss. If your idea can't stand on its own merit, perhaps it needs a bit more thought—or maybe it's just a terrible idea. Persuasion is the true mark of a leader; rank-pulling is the mark of a tyrant (and nobody likes a tyrant).

Scenario: The Rank-Pulling Fiasco

Consider being a CEO who regularly silences dissent by pulling rank, insisting your way is the only way. This might work in the short term, but eventually, the best and brightest will flee, leaving behind yes-men and a company on the brink of collapse.

Example: The Persuasive Leader

Take, for example, the CEO of a growing fashion brand. This CEO often dismissed their team's innovative ideas, resorting to "because I said so" tactics. This approach stifled creativity and drove away the most talented designers who felt undervalued. In contrast, when they began encouraging open discussions and rational debates, the team felt empowered, and the company flourished with fresh, market-leading designs. Lesson learned: Lead with logic, not titles.

CONCLUSION

The journey to successful leadership is not about asserting dominance but about fostering collaboration and trust. As a CEO, recognising the value of your team and creating an environment where everyone feels empowered to contribute is essential. By avoiding the traps of ego-driven leadership, you can navigate the complexities of your role and steer your company toward long-term success.

Additional Reflections

Remember, the role of a CEO is not just to lead, but to inspire and empower those around them. A great CEO understands the value of their team, makes informed decisions, and persuades through reason. By embracing humility, fostering collaboration, and prioritising transparency, you can build a stronger, more resilient organisation capable of achieving sustainable success.

4.
FEEDBACK WITHOUT A LOOP IS AS FUNCTIONAL AS A ROAD THAT LEADS TO A CLIFF EDGE

In the high-stakes world of corporate leadership, feedback is the lifeblood of continuous improvement. Yet, many CEOs overlook the importance of creating a robust, closed-loop feedback system, focusing instead on surface-level metrics. This chapter delves into the pitfalls of ignoring comprehensive feedback mechanisms and highlights how a closed-loop approach can transform your leadership and your company.

KEY PERFORMANCE INDICATORS: THE MIRAGE OF SUCCESS

While Key Performance Indicators (KPIs) are essential for tracking progress and setting goals, an over-reliance on them can blind a CEO to the underlying issues within their team. KPIs become meaningless if your team members are not happy to work with you. A team that's disengaged or undervalued can meet their targets but will lack the innovation and commitment needed for long-term success.

Case Study: The KPI-Obsessed CEO

Imagine a CEO who is laser-focused on hitting quarterly sales targets. On paper, the numbers look great. However, beneath the surface, employees are overworked, undervalued, and increasingly disgruntled. The result? High turnover, loss of institutional knowledge, and a gradual decline in product quality and customer satisfaction. The CEO learns the hard way that KPIs are not the be-all and end-all; the health of the team is equally important. KPIs without happy employees are like a gym membership without the gym—you're not really getting any healthier.

Focusing solely on KPIs can lead to tunnel vision. This CEO missed out on the crucial details that could have indicated brewing dissatisfaction and disengagement among the staff. A drop in creativity, lower problem-solving capabilities, and an increase in errors were all signals missed by an overemphasis on numerical targets.

STAKEHOLDERS VS. SHAREHOLDERS: A BROADER PERSPECTIVE

A common pitfall for many CEOs is the tendency to prioritise shareholders above all else. While keeping investors happy is crucial, it should not come at the expense of other stakeholders, particularly your employees. Remember, everyone, including your staff, are your customers. A company with unhappy staff cannot deliver the excellence required to satisfy shareholders in the long run.

Example: The Disgruntled Workforce

Consider a company where the CEO focuses exclusively on maximising shareholder returns. Cost-cutting measures lead to layoffs, increased workloads, and a toxic work environment. Morale plummets, and productivity follows suit. Eventually, the quality of products or services deteriorates, leading to customer dissatisfaction and, ironically, unhappy shareholders. The lesson? A balanced approach that values all stakeholders, including employees, leads to sustainable success. It's like trying to run a marathon by only eating cupcakes—you might enjoy it initially, but it's not going to end well.

When employees are treated as mere cogs in the machine rather than valued stakeholders, the ripple effects can be disastrous. Unhappy staff can't provide top-notch service, leading to dissatisfied customers. Discontent breeds inefficiency and errors, ultimately impacting the bottom line and leaving shareholders wondering where it all went wrong.

THE ONE-WAY FEEDBACK TRAP

One of the main pitfalls in a company's feedback mechanism is that it only works one way: from managers to employees. This top-down approach can stifle communication and create a culture of fear and compliance rather than innovation and collaboration. To create a truly effective feedback loop, consider getting the staff to evaluate their supervisors and upper management.

Scenario: The Empowered Employee

In a forward-thinking tech firm, the CEO implements a 360-degree feedback system where employees regularly evaluate their supervisors and upper management. This approach fosters an environment of openness and mutual respect. Supervisors receive valuable insights into their leadership style and areas for improvement, while employees feel heard and valued. The result? A self-correcting system that encourages honesty and aligns everyone with the company's goals, preventing the "us vs. them" mentality. It's like having a GPS that actually listens when you say, "No, I don't want to take that left turn!"

Creating a feedback mechanism where the flow of information goes both ways can dramatically enhance organisational cohesion. Employees who feel their voices are heard are more likely to be engaged, committed, and proactive in addressing issues before they become major problems.

CLOSED FEEDBACK LOOP: THE KEY TO AGILITY AND HONESTY

A closed feedback loop breeds honesty and openness, which increases the agility of a company. When staff are not afraid of making mistakes and can raise issues as soon as they arise, the entire organisation becomes more responsive and innovative. CEOs, along with their teams, have more time to come up with well-thought-out solutions, preventing costly knee-jerk reactions.

Example: The Agile Organisation

In a manufacturing company, the implementation of a closed feedback loop leads to significant improvements. Employees are encouraged to report issues and suggest improvements without fear of retribution. When a production problem is identified early by floor staff, it is swiftly addressed through collaborative brainstorming sessions. The company saves time and money by avoiding the escalation of minor issues into major crises. This proactive approach not only enhances product quality but also strengthens team cohesion and trust. It's like having a car with a dashboard that tells you about the problem before you're stranded on the side of the road.

This kind of environment allows for quick pivots and adaptive strategies. When feedback is freely given and received, potential pitfalls are identified and addressed quickly. The organisation becomes a well-oiled machine capable of navigating the complexities of its market with agility and foresight.

CONCLUSION

Feedback without a loop is as functional as a road that leads to a cliff edge. By focusing solely on KPIs, prioritising shareholders over stakeholders, and maintaining one-way feedback mechanisms, CEOs risk driving their companies into the ground. Embracing a closed-loop feedback system, where communication flows both ways and all voices are valued, fosters a culture of honesty, agility, and continuous improvement. This approach not only enhances employee satisfaction and engagement but also drives long-term success for the entire organisation.

Additional Reflections

As a CEO, your role is not just to lead but to listen. By valuing the feedback of your team and creating an environment where everyone feels empowered to contribute, you can navigate the complexities of your role and steer your company toward sustainable success. Remember, the road to success is not a straight line but a loop that continuously evolves through open communication and mutual respect. Think of it as a dance—sometimes you lead, sometimes you follow, but it's always a two-way street.

Incorporating these strategies will help you avoid the pitfalls of ego-driven leadership and create a more resilient, innovative, and harmonious organisation. By closing the feedback loop, you ensure that your company is not only moving forward but doing so with the insight and support of every team member.

5.
NO SUCH THING AS A QUICK DECISION. MIGHT AS WELL FLIP A COIN!

In the fast-paced world of startups and small businesses, the pressure to make quick decisions can be immense. However, the allure of quick wins can often lead to long-term damage. This chapter explores the importance of making informed decisions rather than rushing to impress potential customers or shareholders. Let's dive into the dangers of impulse decisions and the value of thoughtful, informed choices.

THE DANGERS OF IMPULSE BUYS

Rushing to finish a project and impress potential customers can lead to blowing the budget on impulse buys. It's like going grocery shopping when you're hungry—you end up with a cart full of snacks you didn't need. CEOs who overpromise and then scramble to deliver something—anything—often find themselves in this predicament.

Example: The Overpromising CEO

Picture this: A CEO promises a groundbreaking feature to a potential customer without consulting their team. In a rush to deliver, they authorise expensive, last-minute purchases that weren't budgeted for. The result? A strained budget, a stressed team, and a product that's not up to par. Had the CEO communicated properly with the customer and managed expectations, the outcome could have been much more favourable. Instead, the hasty decision leaves the company financially strapped and scrambling to fix issues post-launch.

Humour Insert: Overpromising and underdelivering is a recipe for disaster. The quick win of impressing a customer is overshadowed by the long-term damage to the company's reputation and finances. It's like trying to patch a leaky boat with duct tape—sure, it might hold for a bit, but you're still going to sink eventually.

IMITATING LARGE COMPANIES: PROCESS PITFALLS

Another common mistake is when a startup or small business CEO insists on having lots of processes in place to imitate large established companies but only follows those processes when it suits their agenda. This often happens when the CEO is rushing to deliver on overpromises and pushes their staff to cut corners, ignore processes, and focus on delivering a half-done product.

Scenario: The Selective Process Follower

Imagine a startup where the CEO has implemented numerous processes to mimic larger companies. However, when deadlines loom and overpromises are at risk, the CEO pushes the team to bypass these processes. The result? Incomplete products, missed deadlines, and a disheartened staff who see the double standards. The CEO is quick to blame the team when deliveries are missed, but the staff isn't blind to the root cause. This inconsistent approach is incredibly discouraging and fosters a culture of mistrust and resentment.

Humour Insert: Processes are there for a reason. Ignoring them when convenient undermines their purpose and demoralises the team. It's like having a fire drill plan but ignoring it during an actual fire. Good luck with that.

THE GUT INSTINCT TRAP

CEOs who make decisions based on gut instincts rather than listening to sound advice from their professionals often fall into this trap. While intuition can be valuable, it's not a substitute for informed decision-making. The consequences of ill decisions are real, and having the CEO title doesn't make one immune to them.

Case Study: The Intuitive CEO

Imagine a CEO who regularly ignores the advice of their seasoned team, preferring to go with their gut. This approach might work occasionally, but it's a risky strategy. One particular decision to launch a new product without proper market research backfires spectacularly. Sales flop, and the CEO blames the team for poor execution. However, the team had advised against the launch, citing numerous red flags. The CEO's refusal to listen results in wasted resources, lost credibility, and a demotivated team.

Humour Insert: Blaming your staff for your shortcomings is a very short-sighted strategy and will eventually catch up with you. No amount of gut instinct can replace solid, data-driven decision-making. It's like deciding to navigate a maze blindfolded because you "feel" you know the way—good luck not walking into walls.

EVERY DECISION OPENS A DOOR

Every decision a CEO makes opens a door, and there might be monsters behind some doors. Making informed decisions increases the chances of opening the right doors and steering clear of the monsters. Rushing into decisions can back you into a corner, leaving you with limited and often unfavourable options.

Analogy: The Decision Maze

Imagine navigating a maze where every turn can lead to either treasure or traps. Rushing through the maze without a map or plan is likely to lead you into traps. Taking the time to analyse and choose your path carefully increases your chances of finding the treasure. In business, informed decisions act as your map, guiding you toward success and away from pitfalls.

Humour Insert: Opening the right doors gives you a better chance at success, and this only comes from informed decisions. It's like playing a game of chess—every move counts, and rushing can lead to checkmate in the worst way possible.

CONCLUSION

Quick decisions might seem appealing in the moment, but they often lead to long-term damage. By focusing on informed decision-making, CEOs can avoid the pitfalls of overpromising, cutting corners, and relying solely on gut instincts. Thoughtful, data-driven choices open the right doors and pave the way for sustainable success.

Additional Reflections

As a CEO, the pressure to deliver quick results can be overwhelming, but it's crucial to resist the urge to make hasty decisions. By valuing the input of your team, adhering to established processes, and basing decisions on solid information, you can navigate the complexities of leadership with greater confidence and effectiveness. Remember, it's not just about making decisions; it's about making the right decisions. So, next time you're tempted to flip a coin, take a step back, consult your team, and make an informed choice. Your company's future depends on it.

Humour Insert: Think of decision-making as cooking a gourmet meal. You wouldn't rush it by microwaving everything on high, right? Take your time, follow the recipe, and let it simmer. Your team—and your taste buds—will thank you.

6.
THE MOST IMPORTANT JOB: FIND, DEVELOP AND RETAIN TALENT

In the business world, the true value of a company lies not just in its products or services but in its people. Finding, developing, and retaining talent is arguably the most critical task for any CEO. However, the approach to managing talent has evolved significantly, especially with the changing dynamics of the workforce. This chapter explores how to effectively attract and nurture your most valuable asset—your team—and why it's essential to keep it fun, engaging, and deeply satisfying.

A BUSINESS IS NOT A FAMILY

Let's face it: a business is not a family. It's a business. Everyone who works there does so for financial incentive first and job satisfaction second. Millennials, who now make up the majority of the workforce, aren't interested in working 9 to 5 just to make ends meet. The world is constantly changing, and long gone are the days when people would show up to the office every day, work hard, and endure abuse from managers just to raise a family.

Reality Check: The Modern Workforce

Today's employees value work-life balance and prefer to spend quality time with their actual families rather than their colleagues. Trying to convince people that the business is their family is not only outdated but also quite insulting. Instead, why not make the work satisfying and rewarding enough so they can enjoy their time with their family without worrying about making ends meet or being frustrated about unrealistic expectations at work?

Humour Insert: Think about it: would you prefer to spend your precious hours with someone who calls you "family" but treats you like a servant, or with people who genuinely respect and value your contributions? Exactly.

Example: The Happy Medium

I once worked for a company that tried the "we're a family" approach, but it quickly became clear that this was code for "we expect you to sacrifice personal time without compensation." Employees were burnt out and disengaged. Contrast that with another company that focused on creating a rewarding and balanced work environment. They offered flexibility, recognised hard work, and ensured everyone felt valued. Guess which company retained more talent?

PEOPLE ARE LIKE PLANTS

People are like plants. Pick what you want to grow, look after them, and support them with their needs. Grow them as much as you can, and instead of trying to make them fit your preset job descriptions, develop the jobs around them. They will operate best when they feel comfortable. Forcing people into your preset ideas frustrates them and stifles creativity.

Gardening Analogy: Cultivating Talent

Imagine trying to grow a rose bush in a tiny pot meant for a cactus. It's not going to thrive, and neither will your employees if they're crammed into rigid roles that don't suit their skills and aspirations. When you cultivate talent by providing the right environment, resources, and support, you create a thriving ecosystem where creativity and productivity flourish.

Example: Flexible Roles

I knew a CEO who understood this perfectly. Instead of sticking rigidly to job descriptions, he took time to understand each employee's strengths and passions. When an engineer showed a knack for project management, they shifted his role to include more leadership tasks. The result? The engineer was more engaged, productive, and brought innovative solutions to the team.

PEOPLE LEAVE BAD MANAGERS, NOT BUSINESSES

There's a cliché that goes, "People leave bad managers, not a business." No matter how cliché that sounds, it's true. Many good jobs and opportunities have been lost because of bad managers who enforced their ways, thinking they were superior to everyone else. Even when a team of experts warned them about the consequences of their decisions, they persisted in their misguided ways.

Personal Experience: The Bad Manager Blues

I've left many good jobs because of bad managers. These were individuals who believed their way was the only way, disregarding the collective wisdom of their teams. It's like trying to sail a ship with a captain who ignores the navigator's directions—sooner or later, you're going to hit an iceberg. And trust me, no one wants to be on that sinking ship.

Example: The Micromanager

Consider the story of a talented marketing professional who left a promising position because their manager insisted on micromanaging every aspect of their work. Despite the employee's proven track record, the manager couldn't resist the urge to control. The result? The employee left for a competitor, taking their skills and insights with them, and the original company suffered a significant loss.

THE JOURNEY, NOT THE CHESS GAME

Remember, this is a journey, and everyone within the company should be traveling in the same direction rather than against each other. One common mistake CEOs make is comparing running a business to a chess game where they control each piece. In chess, the pieces aren't aware of each other, but in a business, people are—and they talk to each other.

Communication Breakdown: The Chess Game Fallacy

When a CEO tries to control individuals without telling everyone the direction the company is taking, people start talking and making wild guesses. These guesses almost always lead to thinking the worst because people are naturally risk-averse when work is concerned. It's like trying to drive a bus with all the passengers blindfolded—sooner or later, they're going to panic.

Instead of treating your employees like chess pieces, treat them like fellow travellers on a journey. Share the roadmap, discuss the destination, and make sure everyone knows their role in getting there. When people understand the bigger picture, they're more likely to contribute positively and work together harmoniously.

Example: The Transparent Leader

A CEO I once worked with excelled in this. He held regular all-hands meetings where he transparently discussed the company's goals, challenges, and successes. Employees felt included and informed, which fostered a strong sense of unity and purpose. The open communication made it clear that everyone was working towards the same objectives.

MAKING WORK FUN (FOR REAL)

Saying "It's fun to work here" doesn't actually make it fun. If you want your employees to enjoy working, you need to listen to their needs. Listen properly and actually hear them out. Take their opinions on board. They will spend most of their adult lives working, and sooner or later, they'll realise there's not much point in staying at a company that does not cater to their needs.

Example: Listening to Employees

I once worked for a CEO who prided himself on the company's fun culture. However, the reality was quite different. Employees were overworked, under-appreciated, and the "fun" perks were superficial. It wasn't until the CEO started genuinely listening to employee feedback—addressing concerns about work-life balance, providing growth opportunities, and recognising achievements—that the workplace truly became enjoyable.

Humour Insert: Remember, telling your team it's fun to work at your company is like telling someone they're having a good time at a party when they're clearly not. Actions speak louder than words.

Example: Real Fun

Another CEO transformed his company by incorporating actual fun into the work culture. He initiated flexible working hours, team-building activities that employees actually enjoyed, and a policy of regular breaks to avoid burnout. Listening to what his employees found fun and meaningful made all the difference. The result was a more engaged, happier, and productive workforce.

SEBASTIAN JDEL MONTE

THE MYTH OF LONG HOURS

Long hours and hard work might be necessary at times, especially for startups or new businesses, but thinking this is a sustainable way of working is a common mistake new CEOs make. Don't for a minute think that your staff isn't as committed to the business as you are. Believe it or not, everyone wants to succeed. This does not mean they will spend every waking hour in the office working their asses off.

Reality Check: The Need for Balance

People need time to relax, gather their thoughts, run errands, be with friends and family, and most importantly, have time to themselves. I've worked for CEOs who would tell you off for being five minutes late in the morning while giving you a stern look when you try to leave work even after several hours of overtime. This isn't commitment—it's exploitation.

Humour Insert: Burnout is real, and it's costly. Employees who are overworked and stressed are less productive, more prone to errors, and more likely to leave. Providing a balanced work environment where hard work is appreciated but not abused leads to a healthier, more productive workforce.

Example: The Burnout Factory

In one startup, the CEO believed that the only way to success was through relentless work. Employees regularly worked late into the night and over weekends. Initially, productivity was high, but it wasn't sustainable. Within a year, turnover skyrocketed, and the quality of work plummeted. The company learned the hard way that even the most dedicated employees need time to recharge.

CONCLUSION

Finding, developing, and retaining talent is the most important job for any CEO. By treating employees with respect, providing a supportive environment, and valuing their contributions, you create a thriving, innovative, and loyal team. Remember, a business is not a family, but it can be a place where people feel valued and fulfilled. Listen to your employees, cultivate their talents, and create a culture that truly supports their needs. This is the key to long-term success.

Additional Reflections

As a CEO, your job is not just to lead but to nurture. By focusing on the well-being and development of your team, you can build a stronger, more resilient organisation. Remember, happy employees are productive employees. So, next time you're tempted to cut corners or ignore feedback, think of your team as a garden that needs tending. With the right care and attention, your business will flourish.

Incorporating these strategies will help you avoid the pitfalls of ego-driven leadership and create a more resilient, innovative, and harmonious organisation. By closing the feedback loop, you ensure that your company is not only moving forward but doing so with the insight and support of every team member.

7.
IF YOU ARE RUNNING OUT OF TIME, YOU ARE DOING IT WRONG

One of the most common pitfalls for new CEOs is poor time management, often stemming from unrealistic expectations and improper budgeting. When you assume everything will go according to plan, you're setting yourself up for failure. Nothing ever goes entirely according to plan, especially if you're trying to innovate. Here's why proper time management is crucial and how to avoid the traps that come with poor planning.

THE REALITIES OF DEVELOPMENT: IT TAKES TIME

Developing a service or product takes time—a lot of it. If you insist on your team giving you exact timelines for something that's never been done before and expect them to hit those dates without delays, you're in for a rude awakening. Development isn't like following a recipe; it's more like exploring uncharted territory.

Example: The Unrealistic Timeline

Imagine demanding a team to deliver a new product feature within a month, despite knowing it's a complex task that's never been attempted before. The team, under pressure, rushes through the development process, leading to mistakes and subpar results. As a CEO, you need to recognize that mistakes are an essential part of the development process. Pushing for strict deadlines without allowing room for errors will only lead to frustration and failure. If you can't accept that mistakes are part of growth, it might be time to reconsider your role.

Humour Insert: It's like trying to bake a soufflé for the first time and expecting it to come out perfect. Spoiler alert: it's probably going to collapse.

THE COST OF CUTTING CORNERS

In previous chapters, we discussed the dangers of not following processes, making ill-informed decisions, and pushing people to cut corners. During the development stages, cutting corners will inevitably lead to regret later on. Overlooked mistakes during development can cast long shadows and cause significant issues during certification or deployment stages.

Example: The Corner-Cutting Catastrophe

Consider a tech startup rushing to release a new app. To meet an overpromised launch date, the CEO insists on skipping critical testing phases. The app launches on time but is riddled with bugs, resulting in poor user reviews and a tarnished reputation. The quick win of an on-time release turns into a nightmare as the company scrambles to fix issues post-launch. Restarting the development cycle can be incredibly costly and time-consuming.

Humour Insert: It's like building a house of cards on a windy day and then wondering why it collapsed.

PLANNING: THE UNPREDICTABLE BEAST

All plans fail; the main question is, as a CEO, what will you do about it? If you are planning to the minuscule detail, you will be wasting your time trying to micromanage everything. No plan can be that accurate. If you plan for every little detail, you aren't allowing any time for something to go wrong. Things do go wrong, whether they are in your control or not.

Example: The Exhibition Fiasco

Imagine you're planning to showcase your new product at a major exhibition. Your timeline only allows just enough time for your suppliers to deliver components. If one supplier fails due to unforeseen circumstances, you're left scrambling, blowing your budget on last-minute replacements. A well-thought-out plan includes buffer time for such contingencies.

Humour Insert: It's like trying to get to the airport with just enough time for a perfect trip—then hitting every red light and roadblock possible.

AVOIDING KNEE-JERK REACTIONS

Many CEOs don't allow for reaction time and end up making knee-jerk decisions. These make the CEO look incompetent and over-reliant on their staff to pull long hours and work extremely hard to deliver. As mentioned in previous chapters, this leads to burnout and resentment among staff.

Example: The Knee-Jerk Reaction

A CEO, faced with a missed deadline, demands the team to work overnight to catch up. This last-minute scramble results in exhaustion and further mistakes. The staff grows increasingly frustrated with the lack of foresight and planning. A CEO must build in reaction time to avoid these panic-induced decisions.

Humour Insert: It's like deciding to run a marathon the night before without any training. Good luck not collapsing halfway through.

THE ART OF APPROXIMATION

It's better to be approximately right than precisely wrong. This is especially true for plans. Leave a healthy amount of time in all your plans to account for any uncalculated risks and always keep your customers and staff involved and informed. Customers are more likely to overlook delays when they are aware of the steps of your journey rather than facing nasty surprises.

Example: Communicating Delays

Consider a CEO who regularly updates customers on project progress, including potential delays. When a delay occurs, customers are more understanding because they've been kept in the loop. Conversely, springing a surprise delay at the last minute erodes trust and damages relationships.

Humour Insert: It's like promising your friends you'll be on time for dinner but only telling them you're stuck in traffic after they've been waiting for an hour. Not cool.

CONCLUSION

Effective time management is a critical skill for any CEO, especially in the face of inevitable challenges and unforeseen delays. Rushing to meet unrealistic deadlines, cutting corners, and making impulsive decisions can lead to significant setbacks and long-term damage. Instead, by embracing realistic planning, allowing buffer time for uncertainties, and making informed, data-driven decisions, CEOs can steer their companies toward sustainable success.

Additional Reflections

As a CEO, the pressure to deliver quick results can be overwhelming, but it's crucial to resist the urge to make hasty decisions. Embrace the complexities of development, understand that delays and mistakes are part of the process, and maintain transparent communication with your team and customers. By fostering a culture that values thoughtful planning and informed decision-making, you can build a resilient and adaptive organisation. Remember, it's not just about meeting deadlines; it's about creating lasting value. So, next time you face a time crunch, take a step back, consult your team, and approach the situation with a strategic mindset. Your company's long-term success depends on it.

Humour Insert: Think of time management as crafting a fine piece of art. You wouldn't rush a masterpiece by cutting corners and skipping essential steps. Take your time, plan carefully, and ensure each stroke contributes to the overall vision. Your team—and your company's future—will thank you.

8.
MICROMANAGEMENT - THE WORST KIND

A CEO should be able to look at the bigger picture, whether from a helicopter view or down in the weeds with the rest of the staff. A CEO who cannot communicate this bigger picture and align everyone to this vision is doomed to the biggest mistake of all: micromanaging. Micromanagement frustrates employees, stifles innovation, and ultimately hinders a company's progress. Let's explore why micromanagement is detrimental and how to avoid falling into this trap.

THE BIGGER PICTURE: COMMUNICATE AND ALIGN

As a CEO, your job is to communicate the broader vision and align everyone to this view. Failing to do so leads to micromanagement, as you'll feel the need to control every detail. Your role is to set the direction and let your team navigate. If you find yourself constantly stepping in to correct course, it's a sign that your vision wasn't clear or compelling enough in the first place.

Example: The Frustrated Team

One sure way to frustrate your staff is to control their every move and tell them how to do their jobs. If you need to do this, you either hired the wrong people or have trust issues. Skilled professionals won't put up with this for long. They'll move to a company where they can rely on their training and are trusted to make decisions and deliver their tasks.

Humour Insert: It's like hiring a world-class chef and then insisting on telling them how to chop onions. Guess what? They won't stick around for long before they find a kitchen where they're trusted to do their thing.

MICROMANAGEMENT STIFLES INNOVATION

Micromanagement is the antithesis of innovation. When every decision has to go through the CEO, the process becomes bottlenecked, and creativity is stifled. Employees feel they are not trusted to make decisions, which leads to a lack of ownership and reduced motivation to think outside the box.

Detailed Opinion: Innovation thrives in an environment where people feel empowered to take risks and make decisions. When a CEO insists on controlling every aspect of the business, they send a clear message: "I don't trust you to do your job." This lack of trust is toxic and can quickly spread throughout the organisation, leading to disengagement and high turnover.

Example: The Stifled Team

Consider a tech startup where the CEO reviews and approves every single line of code. Developers, frustrated by the lack of autonomy, stop proposing new ideas and only do what is necessary to get by. The company falls behind its competitors who foster a culture of innovation and trust.

ALIGNING THE COMPANY'S VISION

A common mistake new CEOs make is attempting to align people to the company's vision without including them in its creation. Don't change the vision to fit your agenda. Decide on a vision and include your staff in that decision as they will be taking this journey with you. Value their input. Don't try to change people by force but help them see the vision by reasoning and addressing their concerns.

Example: The Inclusive Leader

Imagine a CEO who sets a vision without consulting their team. The staff feels excluded and uninvested in the company's direction. Conversely, a CEO who involves their team in crafting the vision fosters a sense of ownership and commitment. People will not share their concerns if you don't create a safe environment for them to speak their minds.

Humour Insert: It's like trying to lead a conga line without telling anyone the dance moves. Everyone ends up stepping on each other's toes.

TRUST AND RESPECT: THE FOUNDATIONS OF LEADERSHIP

Hierarchies may work on paper or in the army, but today's young workforce is knowledgeable and has access to endless information. As a CEO, you need to earn their respect. Avoid trying to bullshit them by lying, and once caught, don't rely on hierarchy to enforce your authority.

Detailed Opinion: Respect is earned, not given. The days when a title commanded automatic respect are over. Today's workforce demands transparency and honesty. If you try to deceive them, they will see through it, and you will lose their respect. Once trust is broken, it's incredibly difficult to rebuild.

Example: The Trust-Breaker

Consider a CEO who fabricates facts to push an agenda. The team quickly catches on, losing respect for the CEO. Trust is shattered, and the CEO struggles to regain control. In contrast, transparency and honesty build respect and loyalty.

Humour Insert: Trying to pull rank on a well-informed workforce is like trying to convince a group of tech-savvy teenagers that their old flip phone is better than their smartphone. Good luck with that!

CLEAR GOALS, RESPONSIBILITIES, AND ACCOUNTABILITIES

Not identifying clear goals, responsibilities, and accountabilities makes people feel lost, leading to reduced efficiency. If the CEO fails to set these in place, they will find themselves feeling obliged to micromanage.

Detailed Opinion: Clear goals and responsibilities are the cornerstones of effective management. When employees know what is expected of them and how their work fits into the bigger picture, they are more likely to take ownership of their tasks and perform at a higher level. Conversely, a lack of clarity leads to confusion, inefficiency, and, ultimately, micromanagement.

Example: The Lost Team

A team without clear goals and responsibilities flounders. Productivity drops as team members are unsure of their roles. The CEO, seeing the chaos, steps in to micromanage, creating more frustration. Setting clear, achievable expectations from the start prevents this scenario.

Humour Insert: It's like giving someone a treasure map with no landmarks. They'll wander around aimlessly until you finally have to step in with a GPS.

TRUST YOUR HIRES

If you hired the right people, they can manage themselves as long as they clearly see the road ahead. Think about it: a teacher assigns homework and expects students to complete it independently. The teacher doesn't go to each student's house to supervise. So why would a CEO do it?

Detailed Opinion: Trust is the foundation of any successful team. When you trust your employees to do their jobs, you empower them to take ownership and perform at their best. Micromanagement, on the other hand, erodes trust and stifles initiative.

Example: The Independent Team

A CEO who trusts their team and provides clear guidance fosters a productive, innovative environment. Employees take ownership of their tasks and are motivated to excel without constant oversight.

Humour Insert: Micromanaging your team is like standing over someone's shoulder while they're trying to solve a puzzle. You're not helping—you're just annoying them.

INCENTIVISING GOALS

Ensure every staff member is aware of the company goals, not just on paper but in reality. Make sure the goals are as incentivising for them as they are for you.

Detailed Opinion: Goals are powerful motivators, but only if they are meaningful and aligned with personal incentives. When employees see how their work contributes to the company's success and how they will benefit from achieving these goals, they are more motivated and engaged.

Example: The Motivated Team

A CEO who clearly communicates and aligns company goals with personal incentives ensures everyone is motivated to achieve them. Employees see how their work contributes to the bigger picture and are driven to succeed.

Humour Insert: It's like asking someone to climb a mountain without mentioning the breathtaking view at the top. Once they know about the rewarding sense of achievement, they'll be eager to reach the summit!

CONCLUSION

Micromanagement is the worst kind of management. It frustrates employees, stifles innovation, and ultimately hinders a company's progress. By focusing on the bigger picture, involving your team in the vision, earning respect through transparency, setting clear goals, trusting your hires, and aligning incentives, you can avoid the pitfalls of micromanagement and foster a productive, motivated, and loyal team.

Additional Reflections

As a CEO, your role is to guide, not to control. By empowering your team and providing clear direction, you create an environment where innovation and productivity can thrive. Remember, trust is earned, respect is mutual, and the best leaders know when to step back and let their team shine. So, next time you feel the urge to micromanage, take a step back, trust your team, and watch them exceed your expectations.

Humour Insert: Think of leadership as steering a ship. You're there to set the course and make sure you don't hit any icebergs, not to tell the crew how to mop the deck. Let them do their jobs, and you focus on the horizon.

9.
OVERPROMISE, UNDERDELIVER

In the world of business, there's a cardinal rule that every CEO should live by: never overpromise and underdeliver. This principle is crucial for maintaining trust, credibility, and long-term success. Unfortunately, many CEOs fall into the trap of making grand promises to impress stakeholders, only to find themselves unable to meet those expectations. This chapter explores the dangers of overpromising and underdelivering, and offers strategies for setting realistic goals and managing expectations effectively.

THE PERILS OF OVERPROMISING

Overpromising might seem like a good strategy to win clients, attract investors, or boost morale in the short term. However, the long-term consequences can be devastating. When you fail to deliver on your promises, you erode trust and damage your reputation.

Example: The Startup with Lofty Goals

Imagine a startup that promises to revolutionise the industry with a groundbreaking product. The CEO makes bold claims in investor meetings, assuring everyone that the product will be ready in six months. However, as development progresses, it becomes clear that the timeline was unrealistic. Delays pile up, and the product launches a year late with fewer features than promised. Investors are disappointed, customers are frustrated, and the company's credibility takes a significant hit.

Humour Insert: It's like promising your friends a gourmet dinner and then serving them instant noodles. They won't be back for seconds.

DON'T SELL AN IMPOSSIBLE DREAM

One critical mistake CEOs make is selling a dream that is scientifically or humanely impossible to deliver. Neither your customers nor your staff are stupid enough to fall for it. Overpromising something that defies the laws of physics or basic human capability not only sets you up for failure but also insults the intelligence of those you are trying to convince.

Example: The Impossible Dream

Consider a tech company that promises a fully autonomous flying car within a year. The staff, well aware of the technical and regulatory challenges, knows this timeline is impossible. Customers, initially excited, soon become sceptical as the delivery date approaches with no tangible progress. The result is a loss of trust and credibility.

Humour Insert: It's like promising to deliver a unicorn by next Tuesday. Fun idea, but everyone knows it's not happening.

DON'T SUGARCOAT REALITY

Sugarcoating the truth doesn't change reality. The laws of physics don't bend for anyone. Customers and clients don't want lies; they prefer to be told the truth. Just because the CEO doesn't think the customers will be happy with the truth doesn't justify lying. It's easy to lose track of lies. It's better to tell the truth and pull the bandaid off quickly.

Example: The Brutal Truth

A CEO faces delays in product development but, fearing backlash, tells customers that everything is on track. As the launch date nears, the truth comes out, and the backlash is far worse than it would have been had the CEO been honest from the start. Trust is broken, and the company's reputation suffers.

Humour Insert: It's like telling your dentist you floss every day when you don't. Eventually, the truth will come out, and it won't be pretty.

THE DANGERS OF INFLATED EXPECTATIONS

When a CEO sugarcoats their company's capabilities, they increase the expectations of the customers. If this goes unchecked, these expectations soon become unmanageable. Many CEOs make this mistake, putting themselves and their companies under unnecessary pressure. They end up resenting their staff, and their staff resents them in return. The loss of trust between the staff and CEO leads to a thick, uncomfortable atmosphere in the office. Naturally, nobody wants to work under such conditions.

Example: The Expectations Trap

A software company CEO promises an array of advanced features in the next update, knowing full well the development team is already stretched thin. When the team inevitably fails to deliver on these inflated promises, customer dissatisfaction soars, and internal morale plummets. The office atmosphere becomes toxic, with mutual resentment brewing.

Humour Insert: It's like promising your kids theme-park but ending up at the dentist. Talk about a letdown.

COMMUNICATE PROPERLY WITH CUSTOMERS

Usually, these issues result from not communicating properly with the customer. A CEO shouldn't hide their company's progress from the customer. If communications are done right, the customer will understand that this is a startup and development takes time. They will tag along for the journey and more than likely offer their support, as they want you to succeed too.

Example: The Communicative CEO

A CEO regularly updates customers on the realistic progress of product development. When delays occur, they are transparent about the challenges and the steps being taken to overcome them. Customers appreciate the honesty and remain supportive, understanding the startup's growing pains.

Humour Insert: It's like a road trip where you keep everyone updated on the traffic jams. Sure, it's annoying, but at least they know what to expect.

SETTING REALISTIC GOALS

One of the keys to avoiding the overpromise-underdeliver trap is setting realistic goals. This means being honest about what your company can achieve within a given timeframe and with the available resources.

Detailed Opinion: Setting realistic goals requires a deep understanding of your company's capabilities and limitations. It involves thorough planning, clear communication, and a willingness to push back against unrealistic demands from stakeholders. Realistic goals help build trust and credibility, both internally and externally.

Example: The Pragmatic CEO

Consider a CEO who, instead of promising the moon, sets achievable milestones for product development. By breaking down the project into manageable phases and communicating progress regularly, the CEO builds trust with investors and keeps the team motivated. When the product finally launches, it meets or exceeds expectations, strengthening the company's reputation.

Humour Insert: It's like promising a road trip and actually planning the route, rather than just saying, "We'll get there eventually."

MANAGING STAKEHOLDER EXPECTATIONS

Managing stakeholder expectations is critical to maintaining trust and ensuring long-term success. This involves transparent communication, regular updates, and being honest about potential challenges and delays.

Example: The Transparent Communicator

A CEO regularly updates stakeholders on the progress of a major project. When a significant delay occurs due to unforeseen circumstances, the CEO communicates this promptly, explaining the reasons and outlining the steps being taken to address the issue. By keeping stakeholders informed, the CEO maintains their trust and support, even in the face of setbacks.

Humour Insert: It's like telling your passengers that the flight will be delayed due to turbulence, rather than pretending everything's on schedule until they see the storm clouds.

LEARNING TO SAY NO

A critical skill for any CEO is learning to say no. It's tempting to agree to every request and demand to please stakeholders, but this can lead to overcommitting and underdelivering.

Detailed Opinion: Saying no is not a sign of weakness but a strategic decision to protect the company's interests. It's about prioritising what's important and ensuring that commitments made can be realistically achieved. A CEO who can confidently say no to unrealistic demands demonstrates strong leadership and protects the company's integrity.

Example: The Strategic CEO

A CEO receives a request from a major client for a feature that would require significant resources and potentially delay the product launch. Understanding the risks, the CEO respectfully declines, explaining the potential impact on the overall project. By prioritising the company's strategic goals, the CEO maintains focus and delivers on the original promise.

Humour Insert: It's like saying no to adding extra toppings on your pizza when you know it will just make it soggy and unappetising.

THE IMPORTANCE OF UNDERPROMISING AND OVERDELIVERING

The opposite approach—underpromising and overdelivering—can yield significant benefits. By setting modest expectations and then exceeding them, you can delight stakeholders and build a reputation for reliability and excellence.

Example: The Exceeding Expectations Strategy

A CEO announces a modest timeline for a new product launch, knowing the team can deliver ahead of schedule. When the product launches early and with additional features, stakeholders are pleasantly surprised and impressed. This strategy not only builds trust but also enhances the company's reputation for reliability and excellence.

Humour Insert: It's like telling your friends you're making a simple dinner and then surprising them with a three-course meal. They'll be talking about it for weeks.

CONCLUSION

Overpromising and underdelivering is a trap that can have severe consequences for any business. By setting realistic goals, managing stakeholder expectations, learning to say no, and aiming to underpromise and overdeliver, CEOs can build trust, credibility, and long-term success. Remember, it's better to promise a little and deliver a lot than to promise the world and fall short.

Additional Reflections

As a CEO, your word is your bond. Ensuring that you can deliver on your promises is crucial to maintaining the trust and support of your stakeholders. By being honest about your company's capabilities, communicating transparently, and setting realistic expectations, you can navigate the complexities of leadership with integrity and effectiveness. So, next time you're tempted to make a grand promise, take a step back, assess the situation realistically, and aim to exceed, rather than merely meet, expectations.

Humour Insert: Think of it as promising a backyard barbecue and then surprising everyone with a full-blown luau. Your stakeholders—and your reputation—will thank you.

10.
NEVER LIE!

In the business world, honesty is not just a moral principle; it's a critical component of long-term success. Lying, whether to customers or employees, may offer short-term gains, but it invariably leads to long-term consequences. This chapter explores why honesty is paramount and how lying can undermine everything you've worked to build.

READ THE PREVIOUS CHAPTER AGAIN

Before delving into the details of this chapter, take a moment to revisit Chapter 9. The principles of not overpromising and underdelivering are closely tied to the importance of honesty. Setting realistic expectations and maintaining transparency are crucial steps in avoiding the pitfalls of dishonesty.

Humour Insert: It's like watching a movie sequel without seeing the original—you might get the gist, but you're missing the full story.

THE SHORT-TERM GAIN, LONG-TERM PAIN

Lying might seem like an easy way out when faced with difficult situations, but the repercussions can be severe. Dishonesty can offer immediate relief or advantage, but it inevitably leads to distrust and credibility issues.

Example: The Quick Fix

Consider a CEO who lies about the readiness of a new product to secure a major client. The product is rushed to market, riddled with bugs and incomplete features. The client, feeling deceived, not only cancels the contract but also spreads the word about the company's unreliability. The short-term gain of securing the client quickly turns into long-term damage to the company's reputation.

Humour Insert: It's like putting a band-aid on a leaky dam—it might hold for a second, but you're still going to get soaked.

TRUST IS HARD TO EARN AND EASY TO LOSE

Building trust takes time, effort, and consistent honesty. Once trust is broken, it's incredibly difficult to rebuild. Employees, customers, and investors all value transparency and integrity. When a CEO lies, it undermines the trust that these stakeholders have placed in the company.

Example: The Trust Breach

A CEO lies to employees about the financial health of the company, assuring them that jobs are secure despite impending layoffs. When the truth comes out, employees feel betrayed, morale plummets, and top talent starts to leave. The CEO's attempt to prevent panic backfires, leading to an even worse situation.

Humour Insert: It's like telling your partner you remembered their birthday but then forgetting the gift. Good luck regaining that trust!

THE RIPPLE EFFECT OF LIES

Lies have a way of multiplying. One lie often leads to another, creating a web of deceit that becomes increasingly difficult to manage. This ripple effect can spread throughout the company, affecting culture, performance, and ultimately, the bottom line.

Example: The Web of Lies

Imagine a CEO who lies about a project's progress to buy more time. To cover this lie, they fabricate additional stories, involving more people and creating a complex web of deceit. Eventually, the truth surfaces, leading to a loss of credibility, internal chaos, and a significant setback for the company.

Humour Insert: It's like telling a small lie about eating the last cookie, then needing an elaborate alibi involving a cookie-stealing ghost. It just gets ridiculous.

THE VALUE OF TRANSPARENCY

Honesty and transparency are foundational to a healthy company culture. When CEOs are transparent about challenges, it fosters a culture of trust and collaboration. Employees are more likely to engage and contribute solutions when they feel they are being told the truth.

Example: The Transparent Approach

A CEO facing a major product delay decides to be upfront with both employees and customers. By explaining the reasons behind the delay and the steps being taken to address the issues, the CEO maintains trust and garners support. Employees feel respected and motivated to overcome the challenges, while customers appreciate the honesty and remain loyal.

Humour Insert: It's like admitting you're lost on a road trip and asking for directions. Sure, it's a hit to your pride, but you'll get to your destination a lot faster.

BUILDING A CULTURE OF HONESTY

Creating an environment where honesty is valued starts at the top. CEOs must lead by example, demonstrating integrity in every action and decision. This sets the tone for the entire organisation, encouraging employees to follow suit.

Detailed Opinion: Leading with integrity means being honest even when it's difficult. It involves owning up to mistakes, communicating transparently, and consistently aligning actions with words. This not only builds trust but also fosters a positive and ethical workplace culture.

Example: The Honest Leader

A CEO makes a mistake in a strategic decision and openly admits it to the team. By taking responsibility and discussing the lessons learned, the CEO demonstrates integrity and earns respect. The team feels empowered to be honest about their own mistakes and to focus on solutions rather than cover-ups.

Humour Insert: It's like admitting you can't assemble IKEA furniture without help. Everyone appreciates the honesty, and you get the bookshelf put together without any leftover screws.

CONCLUSION

Honesty is not just a virtue; it's a strategic advantage in business. Lies might offer short-term relief, but they lead to long-term damage to trust, credibility, and relationships. By committing to transparency and integrity, CEOs can build a strong foundation for sustainable success.

Additional Reflections

As a CEO, your actions set the tone for the entire organisation. Embracing honesty and transparency not only builds trust but also creates a culture where employees feel valued and respected. Remember, the truth might be tough to deliver at times, but it's always the best policy in the long run. So, next time you're tempted to bend the truth, think of the bigger picture and choose integrity. Your company—and your conscience—will thank you.

Humour Insert: Think of honesty as the best insurance policy. It might not always be the easiest path, but it's the one that keeps you covered in the long run.

11.
EMBRACE CHANGE AND INNOVATION

Change and innovation are the lifeblood of progress. In a rapidly evolving business landscape, the ability to adapt and innovate is crucial for survival and success. This chapter explores the importance of embracing change and fostering a culture of innovation within your organisation.

THE FEAR OF CHANGE

Change can be intimidating. It disrupts routines, challenges the status quo, and requires stepping out of comfort zones. However, resisting change can be far more damaging. Companies that fail to adapt to changing market conditions, technological advancements, and customer needs risk becoming obsolete.

Example: The Resistant Company

Consider a once-dominant tech company that resisted the shift to mobile computing. While competitors embraced the change, investing in mobile technologies and adapting their strategies, this company clung to its traditional product lines. As a result, it lost market share and struggled to stay relevant in a mobile-first world.

Humour Insert: It's like refusing to upgrade from a flip phone because "it still makes calls." Meanwhile, the world moves on, and you're left behind with your T9 texting.

CREATING A CULTURE OF INNOVATION

Innovation doesn't happen by accident. It requires a deliberate effort to create an environment where new ideas are encouraged, experimentation is welcomed, and failure is seen as a learning opportunity.

Detailed Opinion: Fostering a culture of innovation involves empowering employees to think creatively, providing the resources needed for experimentation, and rewarding innovative thinking. It also means accepting that not all ideas will succeed and that failure is a natural part of the innovation process.

Example: The Innovative Company

A CEO implements an innovation lab within the company, where employees are encouraged to develop and test new ideas. Regular "hackathons" are held, and the best ideas receive funding for further development. This approach not only leads to breakthrough products but also boosts employee engagement and morale.

Humour Insert: It's like turning your office into a playground for grown-ups. Who knows what amazing things people can create when they're having fun?

EMBRACING TECHNOLOGICAL ADVANCEMENTS

Technology is a key driver of change in today's business world. Embracing new technologies can lead to increased efficiency, better customer experiences, and new business opportunities. However, it requires a willingness to invest in learning and adapting to these advancements.

Example: The Tech-Savvy Company

A retail company embraces e-commerce and invests in a robust online platform. By leveraging data analytics, they gain insights into customer behaviour and preferences, enabling them to tailor their offerings and improve customer satisfaction. As a result, they not only survive the shift to online shopping but thrive in it.

Humour Insert: It's like discovering the magic of online grocery shopping. No more wandering the aisles—you get what you need with a few clicks.

THE ROLE OF LEADERSHIP IN DRIVING CHANGE

Leadership plays a crucial role in driving and managing change. CEOs must not only champion innovation but also guide their organisations through the transitions that come with it. This involves clear communication, setting a vision, and providing the necessary support and resources.

Detailed Opinion: Effective leaders understand that change is a journey. They set a clear vision, communicate it effectively, and inspire their teams to embrace the journey. They also recognise the challenges and provide the support needed to navigate them.

Example: The Visionary Leader

A CEO envisions a digital transformation for the company, moving from traditional operations to a cloud-based infrastructure. By clearly communicating the benefits, involving employees in the planning process, and providing training and support, the CEO successfully leads the organisation through the transition, resulting in increased agility and competitiveness.

Humour Insert: It's like being a tour guide in a new city. You show everyone the exciting places, explain why they're worth visiting, and make sure no one gets lost along the way.

CONCLUSION

Embracing change and fostering innovation are essential for long-term success in today's fast-paced business environment. By creating a culture that encourages creativity, leveraging technological advancements, and providing strong leadership, CEOs can navigate the complexities of change and drive their organisations toward a prosperous future. Change might be intimidating, but it's also the catalyst for growth and improvement.

Additional Reflections

As a CEO, your willingness to embrace change and foster innovation sets the tone for the entire organisation. Encourage your team to think outside the box, experiment, and learn from failures. Emphasise the importance of continuous learning and adaptation. Remember, the companies that thrive are those that see change not as a threat but as an opportunity. So, next time you're faced with a choice between the old and the new, take a leap of faith and embrace the future. Your company's success depends on it.

Humour Insert: Think of change as upgrading from a rickety bicycle to a shiny new electric scooter. Sure, there's a learning curve, but the ride is smoother and a lot more fun.

12. BUILDING A RESILIENT ORGANISATION

In a world filled with uncertainties and disruptions, resilience has become a critical attribute for businesses. Building a resilient organisation means creating systems and a culture that can withstand shocks, adapt to changes, and emerge stronger from challenges. This chapter explores strategies for enhancing organisational resilience and highlights approaches that CEOs should avoid to ensure long-term success.

THE IMPORTANCE OF AGILITY

Agility is a key component of resilience. An agile organisation can quickly pivot in response to market changes, customer needs, or unforeseen events. This requires flexible structures, adaptive processes, and a culture that embraces change. However, CEOs should avoid over-centralising decision-making, which can slow down response times and stifle innovation. Empowering managers and teams to make decisions increases agility and ensures a faster, more effective response to changing conditions.

Example: The Agile Retailer

Consider a retail company that swiftly adapts to the pandemic by expanding its online presence and offering curb-side pickup. Their ability to pivot quickly keeps them afloat while competitors struggle. By being agile, they not only survive the crisis but also capture a larger market share.

Humour Insert: It's like being a professional gymnast—able to flip and twist in any direction without breaking a sweat.

DIVERSIFYING RISK

Resilience also involves diversifying risk. Relying too heavily on a single revenue stream, market, or supplier can make a company vulnerable. Diversifying reduces the impact of any single failure and spreads risk across multiple areas. Neglecting to invest in technology can also hinder a company's ability to diversify and adapt. CEOs must prioritise technological advancements to maintain efficiency and flexibility, ensuring the organisation can handle unexpected changes.

Example: The Diversified Manufacturer

A manufacturing company diversifies its supply chain by sourcing materials from multiple suppliers in different regions. When one supplier faces a disruption, the company can quickly shift to another, ensuring continuous production. This strategy minimises risk and enhances stability.

Humour Insert: It's like not putting all your eggs in one basket—because if you trip, it's an omelette disaster.

FOSTERING A STRONG COMPANY CULTURE

A resilient organisation is built on a strong company culture. This includes a sense of purpose, strong values, and a supportive environment. When employees feel connected to the company's mission and each other, they are more likely to pull together in tough times. CEOs should avoid underestimating the importance of culture. A resilient organisation requires a positive, inclusive culture where employees are motivated and engaged. Neglecting culture can lead to low morale and disengagement, especially during tough times.

Example: The United Team

A CEO fosters a strong company culture by promoting teamwork, recognising achievements, and supporting employee well-being. During a financial downturn, the team remains committed and motivated, finding innovative solutions to navigate the crisis. The company emerges stronger due to its cohesive and dedicated workforce.

Humour Insert: It's like having a well-bonded superhero team. When trouble strikes, they unite and save the day.

INVESTING IN CONTINUOUS LEARNING

Continuous learning and development are vital for resilience. Investing in employee training and development ensures that the workforce remains skilled and adaptable to new challenges and technologies. Neglecting employee input and feedback can lead to missed opportunities for improvement and innovation. A resilient organisation values and incorporates input from all levels, ensuring that it is always learning and evolving.

Example: The Learning Organisation

A tech company invests heavily in continuous learning programs, offering regular training and development opportunities. As a result, employees are skilled in the latest technologies and can quickly adapt to industry changes. This continuous learning culture keeps the company competitive and resilient.

Humour Insert: It's like giving your team a steady diet of brain-boosting smoothies. They stay sharp and ready for anything.

SCENARIO PLANNING AND PREPAREDNESS

Proactively preparing for potential disruptions enhances resilience. This involves scenario planning, risk assessment, and developing contingency plans. Being prepared allows a company to respond quickly and effectively to unexpected events. Poor communication during crises can create uncertainty and mistrust. CEOs must prioritise transparent, consistent communication to maintain morale and ensure everyone is aligned with the company's goals.

Example: The Prepared Business

A logistics company conducts regular scenario planning exercises, identifying potential risks such as natural disasters or supply chain disruptions. They develop detailed contingency plans and conduct drills to ensure readiness. When a major disruption occurs, they execute their plan smoothly, minimising impact and maintaining operations.

Humour Insert: It's like practicing fire drills. When the alarm goes off, everyone knows exactly where to go and what to do.

CONCLUSION

Building a resilient organisation is essential for navigating today's unpredictable business environment. By fostering agility, diversifying risk, nurturing a strong company culture, investing in continuous learning, and proactively preparing for disruptions, CEOs can ensure their companies not only survive but thrive in the face of challenges. Avoiding common pitfalls is equally important to sustain these efforts.

Additional Reflections

Resilience is not just about surviving crises; it's about emerging stronger and more adaptable. As a CEO, your role is to build an organisation that can withstand shocks and continue to grow. Emphasise flexibility, invest in your people, and prepare for the unexpected. Remember, resilience is a journey, not a destination. By cultivating a resilient mindset and practices, you can lead your company through any storm and toward a brighter future.

Humour Insert: Think of resilience as having a bouncy castle for a business. No matter how hard you fall, you bounce right back up.

13. THE ART OF EFFECTIVE COMMUNICATION

Effective communication is the backbone of successful leadership. As a CEO, your ability to convey ideas, inspire your team, and foster open dialogue can significantly impact your organisation's success. This chapter delves into the art of effective communication and offers practical tips for enhancing your communication skills. CEOs should avoid relying solely on intermediaries to communicate important messages, as this can lead to misinterpretation and a lack of clarity. Overcomplicating your message with jargon and complex language can alienate your audience and obscure your main points. Additionally, a one-way communication style where the CEO does not listen to employee feedback can lead to disengagement and missed opportunities for improvement. Providing inconsistent information or changing messages frequently can create confusion and erode trust within the team.

CLARITY AND CONCISENESS

Clear and concise communication ensures that your message is understood and remembered. Avoid jargon, be direct, and make sure your key points are easily digestible. This means distilling complex ideas into their simplest form without losing the essence of the message. It also involves structuring your communication in a way that highlights the most important points first, ensuring they are not lost in unnecessary details.

Example: The Clear Communicator

A CEO announces a new strategic initiative in a company-wide meeting. Instead of using complex business jargon, they explain the initiative in simple, straightforward language, highlighting the benefits and the steps involved. Employees leave the meeting with a clear understanding of the plan and their roles in its execution.

Humour Insert: It's like explaining your favourite TV show to a friend—keep it simple and focus on the exciting parts.

ACTIVE LISTENING

Effective communication is a two-way street. Active listening involves fully engaging with the speaker, understanding their message, and responding thoughtfully. It shows respect and fosters a culture of open dialogue. t's not just about hearing the words but also understanding the underlying emotions and intentions. Active listening can help build stronger relationships, resolve conflicts, and enhance teamwork.

Example: The Active Listener

During a team meeting, a CEO listens attentively to employees' concerns and suggestions. By acknowledging their input and asking follow-up questions, the CEO demonstrates that they value their team's perspectives. This approach encourages more open communication and fosters a collaborative environment.

Humour Insert: It's like being a good friend who doesn't just wait for their turn to talk but actually listens and responds.

NONVERBAL COMMUNICATION

Body language, facial expressions, and tone of voice play a significant role in communication. Being aware of your nonverbal cues can enhance the effectiveness of your message. Nonverbal communication can reinforce what is being said, convey emotions, and build trust. It is essential to be mindful of your body language and ensure it aligns with your verbal messages to avoid mixed signals.

Example: The Mindful Communicator

A CEO delivers a difficult message about organisational changes. By maintaining eye contact, using a calm tone, and displaying open body language, they convey empathy and confidence. This nonverbal communication helps reassure employees and ease their concerns.

Humour Insert: It's like using emojis in a text message—they add emotion and clarity to your words.

FEEDBACK AND CONSTRUCTIVE CRITICISM

Providing feedback is an essential part of communication. When done correctly, it can motivate and guide employees toward improvement. Focus on constructive criticism that is specific, actionable, and delivered with empathy. It is important to balance positive and negative feedback to ensure that employees feel valued and encouraged to grow. Constructive feedback should focus on behaviours and outcomes rather than personal attributes.

Example: The Constructive Critic

A CEO provides feedback to a team member on a project. Instead of just pointing out what went wrong, they offer specific suggestions for improvement and highlight what was done well. This balanced approach helps the employee learn and grow without feeling discouraged.

Humour Insert: It's like telling someone their cooking needs more salt—helpful and specific, without crushing their culinary dreams.

REGULAR AND TRANSPARENT UPDATES

Keeping your team informed with regular and transparent updates builds trust and keeps everyone aligned. Share both the successes and challenges the company is facing. Transparency fosters a culture of openness and honesty, which can lead to greater employee engagement and trust. Regular updates help to keep the team informed and involved, reducing uncertainty and speculation.

Example: The Transparent Leader

A CEO holds monthly town hall meetings to update employees on company performance, upcoming projects, and any challenges. By being open and honest, they build trust and keep the team engaged and informed.

Humour Insert: It's like having a family meeting to keep everyone on the same page. Just without the drama of who ate the last cookie.

CONCLUSION

Effective communication is crucial for successful leadership. By being clear, concise, and actively listening, you can foster a culture of open dialogue and collaboration. Remember, communication is not just about speaking; it's about connecting with your audience and ensuring your message is understood and acted upon.

Additional Reflections

As a CEO, your communication skills can significantly impact your organisation's success. Focus on clarity, active listening, nonverbal communication, constructive feedback, and regular updates. By mastering the art of communication, you can inspire your team, build trust, and drive your company toward its goals. So, next time you communicate, remember: it's not just about what you say, but how you say it.

Humour Insert: Think of communication as a recipe. The right ingredients, mixed well, create a dish everyone enjoys. Get it wrong, and you'll leave a bad taste in their mouths.

14.
LEADING BY EXAMPLE

The most powerful tool a CEO has is the ability to lead by example. Your actions, attitudes, and behaviours set the tone for the entire organisation. This chapter explores the importance of leading by example and provides practical strategies for embodying the values and culture you want to instil in your company.

WALKING THE TALK

As a CEO, your actions speak louder than your words. If you expect your employees to adhere to certain values and standards, you must embody those same principles. Leading by example means demonstrating the behaviour you expect from others, consistently upholding the company's values, and maintaining high standards of integrity and accountability.

Avoid: Hypocrisy and Inconsistency

Avoid saying one thing and doing another. Hypocrisy can quickly erode trust and credibility. Ensure your actions align with your words to maintain consistency and trust within your team.

Example: The Integrity-Driven CEO

A CEO who emphasises the importance of integrity and ethical behaviour must also demonstrate these values in their daily actions. By making decisions transparently and ethically, they reinforce the importance of these principles and inspire their team to do the same.

Humour Insert: It's like telling your kids to eat their vegetables while you're munching on a candy bar. They're going to follow what you do, not what you say.

ACCOUNTABILITY AND RESPONSIBILITY

Leading by example also means taking responsibility for your actions and holding yourself accountable. When things go wrong, owning up to mistakes sets a powerful example for your team. This approach fosters a culture of accountability where everyone feels responsible for their contributions and the organisation's success.

Avoid: Blame Shifting and Avoidance

Blaming others for mistakes or avoiding responsibility can damage morale and erode trust. Accepting accountability encourages a culture of honesty and integrity.

Example: The Accountable Leader

After a failed product launch, a CEO takes full responsibility, analyses what went wrong, and shares the lessons learned with the team. This accountability fosters a culture of trust and continuous improvement.

Humour Insert: It's like being the captain of a ship and admitting you missed the lighthouse. It's better than pretending the rocks came out of nowhere.

COMMITMENT AND HARD WORK

Demonstrating commitment and a strong work ethic inspires your team to match your dedication. Show that you are willing to put in the effort and go the extra mile for the company's success. Your visible dedication can motivate employees to invest their best efforts in their work.

Avoid: Laziness and Lack of Dedication

A CEO who is perceived as lazy or disengaged will struggle to motivate their team. Show your commitment through hard work and dedication.

Example: The Hardworking CEO

A CEO regularly stays late to help with critical projects and is always the first to volunteer for challenging tasks. This visible commitment encourages employees to also invest their best efforts in their work.

Humour Insert: It's like being the first one on the dance floor. Once you start busting moves, everyone else will follow.

EMPATHY AND SUPPORT

Empathy is a crucial trait for effective leadership. By showing understanding and support for your employees, you create a positive and inclusive work environment. Empathy helps build strong relationships, fosters collaboration, and enhances overall morale.

Avoid: Ignoring Employee Concerns

Failing to acknowledge or address employees 'concerns can lead to disengagement and dissatisfaction. Show genuine care and support for your team.

Example: The Empathetic Leader

A CEO takes the time to listen to employees 'concerns and offers support during difficult times. By showing empathy, they build strong, trusting relationships with their team members.

Humour Insert: It's like being the team's cheerleader and therapist rolled into one. A little "you got this" goes a long way.

CONTINUOUS LEARNING AND GROWTH

Leading by example also means demonstrating a commitment to personal and professional growth. By continuously seeking to improve yourself, you encourage your team to do the same. Emphasise the importance of learning and development within the organisation.

Avoid: Complacency and Stagnation

A complacent leader who resists change and growth can stifle innovation and progress. Embrace continuous improvement and inspire your team to do the same.

Example: The Lifelong Learner

A CEO regularly attends workshops, reads industry literature, and seeks feedback for improvement. This dedication to learning sets a precedent for the entire organisation to value growth and development.

Humour Insert: It's like being a perpetual student in the school of life. The more you learn, the more you inspire others to hit the books.

CONCLUSION

Leading by example is one of the most effective ways to inspire and motivate your team. By embodying the values and behaviours you wish to see in your organisation, you set a powerful standard for others to follow. Remember, your actions as a CEO are always being watched, and they speak volumes about your leadership.

Additional Reflections

As a CEO, your influence extends beyond policies and directives. Your behaviour sets the tone for the entire organisation. Lead with integrity, accountability, commitment, empathy, and a thirst for learning. By doing so, you create a culture that reflects these values and drives the company toward success. So, next time you think about how to inspire your team, remember that the best way to lead is by example.

Humour Insert: Think of leading by example as being the lead actor in a movie. The cast and crew take their cues from you, so make sure your performance is Oscar-worthy.

15.
BALANCING SHORT-TERM WINS AND LONG-TERM GOALS

In the fast-paced world of business, it can be tempting to focus on short-term wins to impress stakeholders and boost immediate results. However, sustainable success requires balancing these quick victories with long-term goals. This chapter explores strategies for maintaining this balance and ensuring that your company thrives both now and in the future.

THE TEMPTATION OF QUICK WINS

Quick wins can provide immediate gratification and a sense of progress. They boost morale, satisfy stakeholders, and can generate short-term financial gains. However, an overemphasis on short-term results can lead to neglect of long-term strategic planning.

Avoid: Short-Sightedness and Neglect of Strategy

Focusing solely on short-term gains without considering long-term impacts can lead to unsustainable practices. Ensure that your quick wins align with the broader strategic goals of the organisation.

Example: The Short-Sighted CEO

A CEO focuses solely on boosting quarterly sales figures, implementing aggressive discounting strategies that drive immediate revenue but erode profit margins and brand value. Over time, this approach leads to diminished customer loyalty and long-term financial instability.

Humour Insert: It's like eating candy for a quick energy boost and then wondering why you're crashing an hour later. Balance, people!

THE IMPORTANCE OF LONG-TERM VISION

While short-term wins are important, they should not come at the expense of long-term goals. A clear vision for the future provides direction and helps prioritise efforts that contribute to sustainable growth.

Avoid: Lack of Vision and Planning

Neglecting to plan for the long-term can leave the company directionless and reactive rather than proactive. Establish a clear, long-term vision that guides strategic decisions and investments.

Example: The Visionary Leader

A CEO articulates a long-term vision for the company, including strategic investments in research and development, talent acquisition, and market expansion. While these initiatives may not yield immediate results, they position the company for sustained success and industry leadership.

Humour Insert: It's like planting a tree. Sure, it takes time to grow, but eventually, you get shade and fruit. Instant gratification is overrated.

BALANCING ACT: STRATEGIES FOR SUCCESS

Achieving a balance between short-term wins and long-term goals requires strategic planning, disciplined execution, and continuous reassessment. Here are some strategies to help maintain this balance:

1. Set Clear Priorities

Establish clear priorities that align short-term actions with long-term objectives. This ensures that immediate efforts contribute to the overarching vision.

Avoid: Misalignment of Goals

Failing to align short-term actions with long-term objectives can lead to wasted resources and effort. Make sure that every short-term initiative supports the broader strategic plan.

Example: Integrated Planning

A CEO implements a planning process that links quarterly targets to the company's five-year strategic plan. This alignment helps ensure that short-term activities support long-term goals.

Humour Insert: It's like making a to-do list that includes both cleaning the kitchen and building your dream home. Every task should move you closer to the big picture.

2. Invest in the Future

Allocate resources to initiatives that drive long-term growth, such as innovation, talent development, and market expansion. Balancing these investments with short-term needs is crucial for sustained success.

Avoid: Underinvestment in Growth

Neglecting to invest in future growth can leave the company stagnant and unable to compete. Ensure that a portion of resources is always dedicated to long-term initiatives.

Example: Future-Focused Investment

A CEO dedicates a portion of the budget to research and development, even during times of financial strain. This commitment to innovation ensures the company remains competitive in the long run.

Humour Insert: It's like saving for retirement while still enjoying your daily latte. You can have both if you plan wisely.

3. Foster a Culture of Adaptability

Encourage a culture that embraces change and adaptability. This helps the organisation respond to immediate opportunities while staying aligned with long-term goals.

Avoid: Resistance to Change

A rigid, inflexible culture can hinder the ability to seize short-term opportunities and adapt to long-term changes. Foster an environment that values adaptability and resilience.

Example: Adaptive Organisation

A CEO promotes a flexible work environment that encourages employees to innovate and adapt to changing market conditions. This agility allows the company to capitalise on short-term opportunities without losing sight of long-term objectives.

Humour Insert: It's like being able to dance to any music that comes on. Flexibility keeps things interesting and forward-moving.

4. Regularly Review and Adjust

Continuously assess the balance between short-term wins and long-term goals. Regular reviews help identify when adjustments are needed to stay on track.

Avoid: Stagnation and Inertia

Failing to regularly reassess and adjust plans can lead to stagnation and missed opportunities. Keep your strategy dynamic and responsive to changes in the environment.

Example: Strategic Reviews

A CEO holds quarterly strategic reviews to evaluate progress toward long-term goals and adjust short-term tactics as necessary. This ongoing reassessment ensures the company remains aligned with its vision.

Humour Insert: It's like checking the GPS on a road trip. Sometimes you need to make a U-turn to get back on the right path.

CONCLUSION

Balancing short-term wins with long-term goals is essential for sustainable success. By setting clear priorities, investing in the future, fostering adaptability, and regularly reviewing progress, CEOs can navigate the complexities of both immediate and future challenges. Remember, success is not just about the next quarter; it's about the next decade.

Additional Reflections

As a CEO, your role is to steer the company toward both short-term victories and long-term prosperity. This requires a delicate balance and a strategic mindset. Embrace the challenge of balancing these priorities, and you'll guide your company toward lasting success. So, next time you're tempted by a quick win, take a moment to consider its impact on your long-term goals. Your future self—and your company—will thank you.

Humour Insert: Think of balancing short-term and long-term goals as a tightrope walk. It takes skill, focus, and a bit of daring, but the view from the other side is worth it.

16.
THE POWER OF DELEGATION

Effective delegation is a cornerstone of successful leadership. As a CEO, your ability to delegate tasks and empower your team can significantly impact productivity, innovation, and overall organisational health. This chapter explores the power of delegation and offers strategies for mastering this essential skill.

THE IMPORTANCE OF DELEGATION

Delegation is not about offloading tasks; it's about empowering your team to take ownership and grow. By delegating effectively, you free up your time to focus on strategic priorities and develop your team's capabilities.

Avoid: Micromanagement and Control

Micromanaging undermines the purpose of delegation and can stifle your team's creativity and independence. Trust your team to handle tasks without your constant oversight.

Example: The Overburdened CEO

A CEO tries to handle everything themselves, from strategic planning to daily operations. This approach leads to burnout and missed opportunities. By learning to delegate, they can focus on high-impact areas and trust their team to manage the rest.

Humour Insert: It's like trying to juggle flaming torches while riding a unicycle—impressive, but unsustainable.

TRUSTING YOUR TEAM

Trust is the foundation of effective delegation. You hired your team for their skills and expertise, so trust them to deliver. Micromanaging defeats the purpose of delegation and undermines trust.

Avoid: Lack of Trust

Failing to trust your team can lead to low morale and reduced productivity. Empower your team by showing confidence in their abilities.

Example: The Trusting Leader

A CEO delegates a critical project to a trusted manager, providing clear objectives but allowing the manager to determine the best approach. This trust empowers the manager, fosters innovation, and ensures the project is completed efficiently.

Humour Insert: It's like teaching someone to ride a bike. At some point, you have to let go and trust they'll pedal on their own without crashing into a tree.

CLEAR COMMUNICATION AND EXPECTATIONS

Effective delegation requires clear communication and setting expectations. Ensure that the person taking on the task understands what is expected, the deadlines, and any necessary resources.

Avoid: Vague Instructions

Ambiguous instructions can lead to confusion and mistakes. Provide clear, detailed guidance to ensure your team knows exactly what is expected.

Example: The Communicative CEO

A CEO delegates a marketing campaign to their team. They provide a detailed brief, outline key objectives, set clear deadlines, and ensure the team has access to the necessary tools and resources. This clarity leads to a successful campaign and a motivated team.

Humour Insert: It's like giving someone a recipe. They need to know the ingredients, the steps, and the cooking time to whip up a delicious dish.

PROVIDING SUPPORT AND RESOURCES

Delegation doesn't mean abandoning your team. Provide ongoing support and resources to help them succeed. Be available for guidance and feedback, but avoid micromanaging.

Avoid: Abandonment

Leaving your team without support can lead to frustration and failure. Balance delegation with the right level of support and guidance.

Example: The Supportive CEO

A CEO delegates a new product development project to the engineering team. They ensure the team has access to the necessary technology, budget, and training. Regular check-ins help address any issues early, but the CEO allows the team autonomy in decision-making.

Humour Insert: It's like giving someone a treasure map and a compass but letting them find their own way to the treasure. Just don't leave them stranded without any clues.

RECOGNISING AND REWARDING EFFORTS

Acknowledging and rewarding the efforts of your team when they successfully complete delegated tasks reinforces the value of their work and motivates them for future projects.

Avoid: Ignoring Achievements

Failing to recognise achievements can demotivate your team and lead to disengagement. Celebrate successes to maintain morale and motivation.

Example: The Appreciative CEO

After successfully launching a new initiative, a CEO publicly recognises the team's hard work and rewards them with bonuses and additional professional development opportunities. This recognition boosts morale and encourages continued excellence.

Humour Insert: It's like cheering on a teammate who scores a goal. Everyone feels pumped and ready to win the game!

CONCLUSION

Delegation is a powerful tool that enhances productivity, fosters innovation, and develops your team's skills. By trusting your team, communicating clearly, providing support, and recognising efforts, you can delegate effectively and lead your organisation to greater success.

Additional Reflections

As a CEO, mastering the art of delegation is crucial for your effectiveness and your organisation's growth. It's not just about offloading tasks; it's about empowering your team and creating a culture of trust and collaboration. Embrace delegation, and you'll find more time to focus on strategic goals while your team thrives. So, next time you're tempted to do it all yourself, remember the power of delegation and let your team shine.

Humour Insert: Think of delegation as a relay race. Pass the baton with confidence, and your team will cross the finish line together.

17.
NURTURING A POSITIVE COMPANY CULTURE

A positive company culture is the bedrock of employee satisfaction, productivity, and retention. It shapes how employees interact, feel about their work, and contribute to the company's success. This chapter explores the elements of a positive culture and strategies for nurturing it within your organisation.

THE ELEMENTS OF A POSITIVE CULTURE

A positive company culture is built on trust, respect, collaboration, and recognition. These elements create an environment where employees feel valued, motivated, and committed to the company's success.

Avoid: Ignoring Employee Well-being

Neglecting the well-being of your employees can lead to burnout and high turnover. Prioritise their health and happiness to build a sustainable work environment.

Example: The Trust-Based Culture

A CEO fosters a culture of trust by encouraging open communication, involving employees in decision-making, and consistently acting with integrity. This trust creates a supportive environment where employees feel safe to share ideas and take risks.

Humour Insert: It's like having a group of friends who always have your back. When trust is strong, so is the bond.

PROMOTING WORK-LIFE BALANCE

Work-life balance is crucial for employee well-being and productivity. Encouraging a healthy balance shows that you value your employees 'personal lives and helps prevent burnout.

Avoid: Encouraging Overwork

Pushing employees to work excessively can lead to exhaustion and decreased productivity. Promote balance to maintain a healthy, motivated team.

Example: The Balanced Workplace

A CEO implements flexible working hours, remote work options, and generous leave policies. These measures help employees manage their personal and professional lives, leading to higher job satisfaction and reduced stress.

Humour Insert: It's like having a job that lets you bring your dog to work. When life is balanced, everyone's tail is wagging.

ENCOURAGING COLLABORATION AND TEAMWORK

Collaboration and teamwork are essential for a positive culture. Encourage cross-functional teams, open communication, and collaborative projects to foster a sense of unity and shared purpose.

Avoid: Creating Silos

Allowing departments to operate in isolation can hinder communication and collaboration. Break down silos to foster a more integrated team environment.

Example: The Collaborative Company

A CEO promotes regular team-building activities, collaborative workshops, and cross-departmental projects. These initiatives build strong relationships and encourage a spirit of cooperation and mutual support.

Humour Insert: It's like hosting a potluck dinner where everyone brings their best dish. The result is a delicious feast everyone enjoys together.

RECOGNISING AND REWARDING ACHIEVEMENTS

Recognition and rewards are powerful motivators. Regularly acknowledging employees 'hard work and contributions reinforces their value and encourages continued excellence.

Avoid: Overlooking Contributions

Failing to recognise achievements can demoralise employees and lead to disengagement. Celebrate successes to maintain a motivated workforce.

Example: The Appreciative Leader

A CEO implements a recognition program that highlights employees 'achievements through awards, bonuses, and public acknowledgment. This recognition boosts morale and motivates employees to maintain high performance.

Humour Insert: It's like throwing a surprise party for someone's achievements. Everyone loves a good celebration!

FOSTERING CONTINUOUS LEARNING AND DEVELOPMENT

Investing in employees 'growth through continuous learning and development opportunities demonstrates a commitment to their professional advancement and the company's success.

Avoid: Stagnation

Neglecting employee development can lead to stagnation and decreased innovation. Encourage continuous learning to keep your team engaged and forward-thinking.

Example: The Learning Organisation

A CEO creates a learning culture by offering regular training sessions, funding for courses, and opportunities for career advancement. This investment in development keeps employees engaged and equipped with the skills needed for future challenges.

Humour Insert: It's like having a subscription to an endless library of knowledge. The more you learn, the more you grow.

CONCLUSION

Nurturing a positive company culture is essential for attracting and retaining top talent, boosting productivity, and fostering a committed and motivated workforce. By building trust, promoting work-life balance, encouraging collaboration, recognising achievements, and investing in development, CEOs can create a thriving organisational culture.

Additional Reflections

As a CEO, your role in shaping and nurturing company culture cannot be overstated. A positive culture drives engagement, innovation, and success. Embrace these strategies to cultivate a culture that supports and inspires your team. Remember, a happy and motivated workforce is the key to long-term success. So, next time you think about improving your company's performance, start with its culture.

Humour Insert: Think of company culture as the soil in which your business grows. Keep it rich and nourishing, and your organisation will flourish.

18. MANAGING CRISIS AND CHANGE

In today's volatile business environment, the ability to manage crises and navigate change is crucial for any CEO. How you respond to challenges and guide your organisation through transitions can make or break your company's success. This chapter explores strategies for effective crisis management and change leadership.

THE NATURE OF CRISES

Crises come in many forms—financial downturns, public relations disasters, operational failures, or sudden market shifts. Understanding the nature of a crisis and its potential impact is the first step in managing it effectively.

Avoid: Downplaying or Ignoring Crises

Ignoring or minimising the impact of a crisis can lead to disastrous outcomes. Acknowledge issues promptly to prevent escalation.

Example: The Financial Crisis

A CEO faces a sudden financial downturn due to market changes. By promptly assessing the situation, communicating transparently with stakeholders, and implementing a strategic recovery plan, they navigate the company through the crisis, emerging stronger.

Humour Insert: It's like dealing with a sudden rainstorm during a picnic. With a quick setup of umbrellas and a dash to the covered area, the fun continues despite the downpour.

CRISIS MANAGEMENT STRATEGIES

Effective crisis management involves preparation, communication, decisive action, and learning from the experience. Here are key strategies for managing crises:

1. Preparation and Planning

Develop a crisis management plan that includes risk assessment, contingency plans, and clear roles and responsibilities. Regularly update and practice these plans.

Avoid: Lack of Preparation

Failing to prepare for potential crises can leave your organisation vulnerable. Plan ahead to mitigate risks.

Example: The Prepared Organisation

A CEO ensures that the company has a comprehensive crisis management plan in place. Regular drills and updates keep the team prepared for various scenarios, minimising the impact of any crisis.

Humour Insert: It's like having a fire drill. You hope you never need it, but when you do, everyone knows exactly where to go and what to do.

2. Clear and Transparent Communication

During a crisis, clear and transparent communication is critical. Keep stakeholders informed about the situation, the steps being taken, and any changes to the plan.

Avoid: Poor Communication

Withholding information or failing to communicate clearly can exacerbate the crisis. Maintain open lines of communication.

Example: The Communicative Leader

A CEO facing a product recall communicates openly with customers, explaining the issue, the recall process, and the measures being taken to prevent future problems. This transparency maintains customer trust and loyalty.

Humour Insert: It's like giving play-by-play commentary during a sports game. Everyone knows what's happening and stays engaged.

3. Decisive Action

During a crisis, swift and decisive action is essential. Assess the situation, make informed decisions, and act promptly to mitigate damage and address the root cause.

Avoid: Indecisiveness

Hesitating to make decisions can worsen the crisis. Act quickly and confidently to manage the situation.

Example: The Decisive CEO

When a cybersecurity breach occurs, a CEO immediately assembles a response team, shuts down affected systems, communicates with customers about the breach, and implements enhanced security measures. This quick response minimises data loss and rebuilds customer confidence.

Humour Insert: It's like dealing with a kitchen fire. Don't just stand there—grab the extinguisher and put it out before the whole house goes up in flames.

4. Learning from the Crisis

Every crisis provides an opportunity to learn and improve. Conduct a thorough post-crisis analysis to identify what went wrong, what worked well, and how to enhance future responses.

Avoid: Failing to Learn

Not analysing and learning from a crisis can lead to repeated mistakes. Use each crisis as a learning opportunity.

Example: The Reflective Leader

After navigating a supply chain disruption, a CEO conducts a review with the team to analyse the response. They identify areas for improvement and implement new strategies to enhance supply chain resilience. This continuous learning approach strengthens the company's ability to handle future crises.

Humour Insert: It's like reviewing game footage after a big match. Analyse the plays, learn from mistakes, and come back stronger for the next game.

LEADING THROUGH CHANGE

Change is inevitable in business, and effective change management is crucial for long-term success. Whether it's a strategic pivot, organisational restructuring, or adopting new technologies, leading through change requires clear vision, communication, and support.

THE ROLE OF VISION

A clear vision provides direction and purpose during times of change. Articulate the reasons for the change, the benefits it will bring, and how it aligns with the company's long-term goals.

Avoid: Lack of Vision

Without a clear vision, change initiatives can flounder. Provide a compelling vision to guide your team.

Example: The Visionary Leader

A CEO leads a digital transformation initiative, clearly communicating the vision of becoming a tech-driven company. They outline the benefits, such as improved efficiency and customer satisfaction, and how the change supports the company's growth strategy. This clarity helps the team embrace the transformation.

Humour Insert: It's like convincing your friends to go on a road trip. Share the exciting destination and the fun stops along the way to get everyone on board.

COMMUNICATION AND INVOLVEMENT

Effective communication and involving employees in the change process are critical. Keep the team informed, address their concerns, and involve them in planning and implementation.

Avoid: Top-Down Imposition

Imposing change without employee involvement can lead to resistance. Engage your team in the process.

Example: The Inclusive Leader

A CEO announces a company-wide restructuring and holds town hall meetings to explain the changes, answer questions, and gather feedback. By involving employees in the process, the CEO reduces resistance and fosters a sense of ownership and commitment.

Humour Insert: It's like planning a surprise party with everyone's input. The more involved they are, the more excited they'll be.

PROVIDING SUPPORT

Support your team through the change by providing the necessary resources, training, and encouragement. Acknowledge the challenges and offer assistance to help employees adapt.

Avoid: Neglecting Support

Failing to support your team during transitions can lead to frustration and disengagement. Offer guidance and resources to ease the process.

Example: The Supportive CEO

During a major system upgrade, a CEO ensures that employees receive comprehensive training and access to support resources. Regular check-ins and positive reinforcement help the team navigate the transition smoothly.

Humour Insert: It's like giving someone a manual and a toolbox when they're assembling a complex piece of furniture. A little support goes a long way in preventing frustration.

CONCLUSION

Managing crises and leading through change are critical skills for any CEO. By preparing effectively, communicating transparently, acting decisively, and learning from experiences, you can navigate crises successfully. Similarly, by articulating a clear vision, involving your team, and providing support, you can lead your organisation through change with confidence and resilience.

Additional Reflections

As a CEO, your ability to handle crises and guide your team through change defines your leadership. Embrace these challenges as opportunities to strengthen your organisation and build a more resilient, adaptable company. Remember, in the face of adversity, your leadership can turn challenges into triumphs. So, the next time a crisis hits or change looms, take a deep breath, communicate clearly, act decisively, and lead your team with confidence.

Humour Insert: Think of managing crises and change as surfing. The waves might be daunting, but with skill and balance, you can ride them to shore and even enjoy the ride.

19.
THE TOXICITY OF GOSSIP AND DIVISION

Creating a positive and productive workplace culture is paramount for any successful organisation. However, certain negative behaviours can quickly undermine this goal. This chapter explores why bad-mouthing personnel and dividing teams to conquer them are detrimental to a healthy work environment and how CEOs can avoid these pitfalls.

THE DANGERS OF GOSSIP AND BAD-MOUTHING PERSONNEL

Gossiping about colleagues or bad-mouthing personnel can have devastating effects on workplace morale and trust. When leaders engage in or tolerate gossip, it sets a negative tone and encourages a culture of backstabbing and mistrust.

Key Points:

Erodes Trust: When employees hear leaders gossiping, they lose trust in management. They begin to wonder what is said about them behind their backs, leading to a pervasive sense of insecurity.

Reduces Morale: Negative talk spreads quickly and can severely damage team morale. It creates an atmosphere of negativity and fear, which hampers productivity and creativity.

Promotes a Toxic Culture: Gossip fosters a toxic environment where employees are more focused on office politics than on their work. This can lead to high turnover rates and difficulty in attracting new talent.

Humour Insert: It's like trying to row a boat with holes in it—everyone's too busy bailing water to actually move forward.

Example: The Gossiping CEO

Imagine a CEO who regularly pulls one employee aside to gossip about another. Over time, this behaviour becomes known throughout the company. Employees start to mistrust the CEO and each other, productivity declines, and the best talent begins to leave for a more supportive environment.

Humour Insert: It's like trying to organise a surprise party, but everyone knows about it and no one's excited.

THE PITFALL OF DIVIDING TO CONQUER

Some leaders believe that dividing their teams and micromanaging them can help maintain control. This strategy, often referred to as "divide and conquer," is not only outdated but also highly counterproductive.

Key Points:

Creates Unnecessary Competition: Dividing teams can create a competitive rather than a collaborative environment. Employees may become more focused on outperforming each other than on achieving common goals.

Destroys Team Cohesion: Effective teamwork requires trust and cooperation. Dividing teams undermines these qualities, leading to a fractured organisation where communication breaks down and projects suffer.

Difficult to Change: Once a culture of division and micromanagement is established, it is challenging to reverse. Employees become accustomed to a lack of collaboration and may resist efforts to change the culture.

Humour Insert: It's like trying to play a symphony with each musician in a separate room—everyone's playing their part, but it sounds like a disaster.

Example: The Divisive Leader

Consider a leader who splits departments into competing factions, believing that this will increase productivity. Instead, it leads to silos, poor communication, and a toxic work environment. Employees become disillusioned, and the company's overall performance suffers.

Humour Insert: It's like hosting a potluck where everyone brings dessert—fun for a moment, but not sustainable for the long term.

BUILDING A POSITIVE CULTURE

To avoid these pitfalls, CEOs must focus on fostering a positive, inclusive culture where trust and collaboration are prioritised.

Promoting Positive Communication

Lead by Example: As a CEO, demonstrate positive communication. Praise publicly and criticise privately. Address issues directly with those involved rather than gossiping.

Encourage Open Dialogue: Create an environment where employees feel safe to voice their concerns and ideas without fear of gossip or retribution.

Example: The Trust-Based Culture

A CEO fosters a culture of trust by encouraging open communication, involving employees in decision-making, and consistently acting with integrity. This trust creates a supportive environment where employees feel safe to share ideas and take risks.

Humour Insert: It's like being on a team where everyone's got your back—you're more willing to try new things and push boundaries.

FOSTERING COLLABORATION

Team-Building Activities: Invest in team-building activities that encourage employees to work together and build trust.

Cross-Functional Projects: Encourage projects that require collaboration across different departments to break down silos and promote unity.

Humour Insert: It's like organising a group project where everyone actually does their part—suddenly, miracles happen.

Example: The Collaborative Company

A CEO promotes regular team-building activities, collaborative workshops, and cross-departmental projects. These initiatives build strong relationships and encourage a spirit of cooperation and mutual support.

Humour Insert: It's like getting everyone to sing in harmony—when it works, it's music to everyone's ears.

CONCLUSION

Gossiping about colleagues and dividing teams are behaviours that can quickly erode trust and create a toxic work environment. By focusing on positive communication and fostering collaboration, CEOs can build a supportive, productive culture where employees feel valued and motivated. Remember, the way leaders communicate and manage their teams sets the tone for the entire organisation. Choose positivity and collaboration over negativity and division.

Humour Insert: Think of a positive work culture as the secret sauce to a great dish. Without it, everything's bland and unappetising.

By embracing these strategies, you'll create a workplace where employees are not only productive but also happy and engaged.

20.
LEADING WITH RESPECT AND INTEGRITY

Respect and integrity are fundamental to effective leadership. How a CEO interacts with their team can significantly impact morale, productivity, and the overall culture of the organisation. This chapter focuses on why shaming personnel, putting them on the spot, and leading them into uncomfortable commitments are detrimental practices, and offers guidance on fostering a respectful and supportive work environment.

NEVER SHAME PERSONNEL

Shaming an employee, whether in private or in front of others, is a destructive practice. It undermines their confidence, damages morale, and can have long-lasting negative effects on their performance and well-being.

Erodes Trust and Confidence: Shaming an employee can severely damage their self-esteem and trust in leadership. It creates an environment of fear rather than one of growth and learning.

Reduces Productivity: Employees who are shamed may become disengaged and less productive, fearing further humiliation rather than focusing on their tasks.

Fosters a Toxic Culture: Regularly shaming employees sets a negative precedent, leading to a culture of blame and anxiety instead of one of support and collaboration.

Humour Insert: It's like trying to coach a basketball team by yelling at players for every missed shot—they're too scared to even try again.

Example: The Respectful Correction

Imagine a CEO who notices an employee struggling with their performance. Instead of shaming them in front of their peers, the CEO arranges a private meeting to discuss the issues. They offer constructive feedback and resources to help the employee improve. The employee feels supported and is more likely to put in the effort to enhance their performance.

Humour Insert: It's like teaching someone to ride a bike—you encourage them when they wobble instead of laughing at their falls.

AVOID PUTTING EMPLOYEES ON THE SPOT

Putting an employee on the spot during a meeting or public forum can create resentment and stress. This practice is often counterproductive and can lead to a lack of engagement and trust.

Creates Resentment: Publicly putting someone on the spot can make them feel singled out and embarrassed, leading to resentment towards management.

Increases Stress: Employees may feel undue pressure and anxiety, which can negatively impact their performance and overall mental health.

Discourages Open Communication: When employees fear being put on the spot, they may be less likely to speak up or share ideas in the future.

Humour Insert: It's like asking someone to dance in front of a crowd without music—they're likely to freeze up or stumble.

Example: The Private Inquiry

Consider a CEO who needs an update on a project but avoids putting the project lead on the spot during a team meeting. Instead, they have a one-on-one discussion to understand the status and any challenges faced. This approach fosters a sense of respect and support, encouraging honest and open communication.

Humour Insert: It's like asking for directions when lost—better done quietly than shouting it across the street.

AVOID LEADING QUESTIONS TO FORCE COMMITMENTS

Asking leading questions in front of others to pressure employees into commitments they're uncomfortable with is not only unfair but also unethical. It undermines trust and can lead to poor decision-making.

Undermines Trust: Employees who feel coerced into commitments may distrust management and feel manipulated.

Leads to Poor Decisions: Forced commitments can result in hasty, poorly thought-out decisions that may not be in the best interest of the employee or the company.

Damages Morale: This practice can create a hostile work environment where employees feel cornered and unsupported.

Humour Insert: It's like asking someone to marry you over a loudspeaker in a crowded mall—awkward and likely to backfire.

Example: The Supportive Discussion

Imagine a CEO who wants an employee to take on a new responsibility. Instead of leading them into a public commitment, they discuss it privately, exploring the employee's concerns and ensuring they have the resources and support needed to succeed. This approach builds trust and encourages employees to take on new challenges willingly.

Humour Insert: It's like proposing a big idea over a quiet coffee—much more likely to get a thoughtful and positive response.

CONCLUSION

Effective leadership is rooted in respect and integrity. By avoiding practices like shaming employees, putting them on the spot, and forcing commitments through leading questions, CEOs can foster a supportive and positive work environment. Treating employees with respect encourages trust, boosts morale, and enhances overall productivity.

Humour Insert: Think of leading with respect as planting seeds in a garden. With proper care and nurturing, you'll see your organisation flourish beautifully.

By embracing these principles, you'll create a workplace where employees feel valued, respected, and motivated to perform at their best. This approach not only benefits individual employees but also contributes to the long-term success and health of the organisation.

21.
LESSONS LEARNED: A CEO'S GUIDE TO ANYWHERE

As we reach the final chapter of this book, it's time to distill the key lessons from each chapter into a concise guide. These lessons will serve as a roadmap for aspiring and current CEOs, helping them navigate the complexities of leadership with confidence, integrity, and effectiveness.

Embrace Continuous Learning

Key Takeaway: Always strive for self-improvement and learning.

Action: Stay curious, seek mentorship, and invest in personal and professional growth. The more you know, the better equipped you are to lead your organisation.

Understand the Value of Your Title

Key Takeaway: Leadership is earned through actions, not just titles.
Action: Demonstrate integrity, capability, and a commitment to excellence. Lead by example to earn the respect and trust of your team.

Avoid Ego-Driven Leadership

Key Takeaway: Ego-driven leadership alienates employees and breeds dishonesty.

Action: Foster a collaborative and inclusive leadership style. Value input from all team members and encourage open communication.

Implement a Closed Feedback Loop

Key Takeaway: Feedback should flow in both directions.

Action: Establish a system where employees can evaluate their supervisors and share their insights. This encourages honesty and continuous improvement.

Make Informed Decisions

Key Takeaway: Quick decisions can lead to long-term damage.

Action: Base your decisions on data and sound advice from your team. Take the time to evaluate options thoroughly before acting.

Focus on Talent Management

Key Takeaway: Finding, developing, and retaining talent is crucial.

Action: Invest in your employees 'growth, recognise their achievements, and ensure they feel valued. Create a supportive and rewarding work environment.

Master Time Management

Key Takeaway: Proper planning prevents poor performance.

Action: Allocate sufficient time for development and account for potential setbacks. Avoid making knee-jerk decisions that can lead to bigger problems.

Avoid Micromanagement

Key Takeaway: Micromanagement stifles innovation and demotivates employees.

Action: Trust your team to do their jobs. Provide clear goals and expectations, and then step back to let them work independently.

Don't Overpromise and Underdeliver

Key Takeaway: Honesty and realistic goal-setting build trust.

Action: Set achievable goals and communicate transparently with stakeholders. Underpromise and overdeliver to exceed expectations.

Always Be Honest

Key Takeaway: Lying erodes trust and credibility.

Action: Maintain transparency with your team and customers. Build a culture of honesty and integrity to foster long-term success.

Embrace Change and Innovation

Key Takeaway: Adaptability is key to long-term success.

Action: Encourage innovation and be open to change. Embrace new ideas and technologies to stay competitive.

Build Organisational Resilience

Key Takeaway: Resilience helps navigate uncertainties and disruptions.

Action: Foster agility, diversify risks, and build a strong company culture. Prepare for potential crises with comprehensive plans.

Communicate Effectively

Key Takeaway: Clear and open communication is essential.

Action: Be concise, listen actively, and communicate transparently. Ensure your team is informed and aligned with the company's goals.

Lead by Example

Key Takeaway: Your actions set the tone for the entire organisation.

Action: Demonstrate the values and behaviours you expect from your team. Lead with integrity, accountability, and empathy.

Balance Short-Term Wins and Long-Term Goals

Key Takeaway: Sustainable success requires a balance.

Action: Set clear priorities that align short-term actions with long-term objectives. Invest in the future while achieving immediate goals.

Delegate Effectively

Key Takeaway: Empowering your team enhances productivity and growth.

Action: Trust your team, communicate clearly, and provide support. Recognise and reward their efforts to build a motivated workforce.

Nurture a Positive Company Culture

Key Takeaway: A positive culture drives engagement and success.

Action: Build trust, promote work-life balance, encourage collaboration, and recognise achievements. Foster continuous learning and development.

Manage Crises and Lead Through Change

Key Takeaway: Effective crisis management and change leadership are crucial.

Action: Prepare for crises with thorough planning, communicate transparently, act decisively, and learn from experiences. Lead your team through change with a clear vision and support.

Avoid Bad-Mouthing Personnel

Key Takeaway: Gossiping about colleagues promotes a toxic culture.

Action: Avoid pulling individuals aside to gossip about others. Focus on building a supportive and respectful environment.

Conquer Toxic Divisions

Key Takeaway: Dividing teams to control and micromanage creates a toxic atmosphere.

Action: Foster unity and collaboration instead of division. Promote a culture where everyone feels comfortable and valued.

Never Shame Personnel

Key Takeaway: Shaming employees, especially publicly, is detrimental.

Action: Guide your staff to improve without resorting to shaming. Provide constructive feedback privately.

Avoid Public Shaming

Key Takeaway: Putting employees on the spot in front of others creates resentment.

Action: Address performance issues privately to avoid embarrassing your staff and fostering a hostile environment.

Don't Use Leading Questions to Corner Employees

Key Takeaway: Leading questions to force commitments can backfire.

Action: Encourage open and honest communication. Avoid manipulating employees into agreeing to uncomfortable tasks.

CONCLUSION

As a CEO, your journey is filled with challenges and opportunities. By embracing these lessons and incorporating them into your leadership approach, you can navigate the complexities of your role with confidence and integrity. Remember, effective leadership is about continuous learning, fostering a positive culture, and empowering your team to achieve shared goals. Lead with honesty, adapt to change, and always strive for excellence. Your success and that of your organisation depend on it.

22.
MOST IMPORTANTLY, ENJOY IT—AFTER ALL, THIS IS YOUR JOURNEY

As we conclude this guide, it's crucial to remember that while starting and running a business is filled with risks and challenges, it's also an exciting journey. This chapter focuses on the importance of finding joy in the process, even when faced with difficulties. After all, this is your journey—make sure you enjoy it.

REMEMBER WHY YOU CHOSE THIS PATH

Starting a new business comes with a lot of risk and frightening experiences, but remember why you chose to do this. It shouldn't be all pain and no gain. Your passion and vision are the driving forces behind your business. They fuel your determination and creativity. When the going gets tough, remind yourself of the reasons you embarked on this journey.

Avoid: Losing Sight of Your Passion

In the daily grind, it's easy to get bogged down by challenges and lose sight of your initial passion. Don't let the stress overshadow your dreams and goals.

Example: The Passionate Entrepreneur

A CEO faced with numerous obstacles reminds themselves of the initial vision and excitement that led them to start the business. By revisiting their goals and the impact they hope to make, they reignite their passion and approach problems with renewed energy.

Humour Insert: It's like hiking up a mountain. The climb is tough, but the view from the top—where you remember why you started—is absolutely worth it.

KEEP THINGS LIGHT, EVEN IN DIFFICULT TIMES

Facing difficult times is inevitable in business. Stress can make situations seem worse than they are, but a bit of humour can lighten the road. Maintaining a light-hearted approach helps you navigate through challenges with a positive mindset.

Avoid: Letting Stress Overwhelm You

Allowing stress to dominate your thoughts and actions can cloud your judgment and exacerbate problems. Aim to keep a balanced perspective.

Example: The Light-Hearted Leader

During a stressful product launch, a CEO encourages the team to take short breaks, share light moments, and celebrate small wins. This approach reduces stress and keeps morale high, making it easier to tackle challenges effectively.

Humour Insert: It's like trying to solve a jigsaw puzzle. If you get too frustrated, take a step back, have a laugh, and come back with a fresh perspective.

HUMOUR IS YOUR FRIEND

Humour is a powerful tool in leadership. It fosters a positive work environment, strengthens team bonds, and makes the journey enjoyable. By keeping things light, you create a culture where creativity and productivity can flourish.

Avoid: Taking Everything Too Seriously

A serious, overly rigid approach can stifle creativity and make the work environment tense. Embrace humour to keep the atmosphere light and engaging.

Example: The Humorous CEO

A CEO who integrates humour into meetings and communications fosters a more relaxed and innovative workplace. Employees feel more comfortable sharing ideas and taking risks, leading to greater innovation and collaboration.

Humour Insert: It's like adding a splash of colour to a black-and-white sketch. A little humour can make everything more vibrant and enjoyable.

CONCLUSION

While the journey of building and running a business is filled with challenges, it's also an adventure filled with opportunities for growth, creativity, and fulfilment. By remembering why you chose this path, keeping things light even during tough times, and embracing humour, you can ensure that your journey is not only successful but also enjoyable.

Additional Reflections

As a CEO, your approach to challenges and your ability to maintain a positive outlook can significantly impact your team and the overall success of your business. Embrace the journey with joy and light-heartedness. After all, this is your story—make it a good one.

Humour Insert: Think of your business journey as a road trip. There will be bumps along the way, but with good music, great company, and a sense of humour, the ride will be a lot more enjoyable. So buckle up, keep smiling, and enjoy the adventure!

About the Author

Sebastian J Del Monte - Obviously this is a pen name as it would not be wise to reveal one's identity in case an ungrateful boss finds out I have written this book and decides to retaliate. Now, isn't this a brilliant example of the fear culture most CEOs or bosses employ to try and control their employees?

www.ingramcontent.com/pod-product-compliance
Lightning Source LLC
Chambersburg PA
CBHW071921210526
45479CB00002B/499